Foreword by Anita Jo Mal'akhim

Roaring All The Day Long

I Kept Silence

Prophetess O.W. Petcoff

Roaring All The Day Long: I Kept Silence
Book Two in the *Roaring All the Day Long* Series
2nd edition

First Printing 2010
ISBN: 978-0-9701184-2-4/0970118422

Published by:
ONOMA Ministries & Publications
Arlington, Texas
omonpee.petcoff@outlook.com
(817) 654-3496

Cover illustrations by Elijah Tan.

Dedication

This book is dedicated to Missionary Genieve (R.T.) Denson. I am thankful for the opportunity to have gotten to know you, even if it were only for a short time before God called you home. I am honored that you chose me to carry on your works via getting your writings to the people. Thank you for being a forerunner for women in ministry such as myself. I love you and miss you, but I know that I will see you again on the other side.

Acknowledgements

Once again, I would like to begin by thanking God for the grace and strength for this undertaking. I am honored that He, The Omnipotent Creator of All Existence, would bestow upon me the awesome responsibility of teaching His People.

To Ron, we did it again! Thanks for your research assistance with this book. You are such a wonderful husband and Man of God. Thank you for loving me.

To Anita Jo Kliewer-Mal'akhim of Mal'akhim Ministries, thank you for agreeing so graciously to write the foreword for this book. I am so thankful that God brought us together during our time in the Masters program at the University of North Texas at Denton. It was a Divine Connection! Thanks for being there for me, Woman of God. May He richly bless and keep you!

To Phyllis Petcoff, my mother-in-law, I appreciate all that you did for me during my time of illness. Your generosity, listening and mothering really touched my heart. I love you!

To Adrian D. Thornton, thank you, my sister, for allowing me to share your story with the rest of the world. You are such an inspiration to me. I love you!

To my sister, Sonya Beard-Adrian, I have said this before but wanted to immortalize my expressions of gratitude to you in the pages of this book. Thank you for being available during my time of need. Your act of kindness helped me to get my much-needed surgery. Thanks for enabling me to write by helping to set in motion the steps to my healing. I love and appreciate you.

To Mrs. Ruth Harper, words cannot express my gratitude for your friendship, wisdom and caretaking. Thank you for being there for me when I needed you. Your nurturing played no small part in my recovery and in my having the strength to get up and write. I love you!

Finally, to each and every one who has helped me throughout the years, please know that you are not forgotten. Although time and space will not allow me to mention each one of you by name, you are forever in my thoughts and prayers.

Table of Contents

Foreword

Several years ago, in our first conversation together, Omonpee (Prophetess O.W. Petcoff) and I were expounding the greatness of God. Much to our delight, the Holy Spirit was quick to join us! I knew then that the Lord called her "His daughter" and that she had been called to a great work in "Daddy's business." As His prophet and scribe, she is a "living epistle." She is an example, a trail breaker/blazer – offering others the opportunity to follow the straight and narrow path to the Lord. "Be careful!" "Walk this way."

About the same time we met each other, the Lord told a friend of mine, "Batten down the hatches, check the bilge pump, throw everything overboard that you don't need. The quickest way through the storm is straight through the middle!" This was followed a few years later by a particularly violent outbreak of spring tornadoes in the North Texas region. Night after night and several times within the same night, strong winds, torrential rain, and hail pelted the region. My friend paced the floor, crying out for God's mercy on her little house; a camper. In God's mercy and grace she received instant peace that passes all understanding when He replied, "Jesus was asleep in the bow of the boat."

There is little room for doubt that Prophetess Omonpee has spent time in rough seas in the bow of the boat. Yet, she has also clearly spent time in the warm and loving embrace of Jesus. How else could one obtain such knowledge and vision for building up the body of Christ? This second book in a series, *I Kept Silence,* provides opportunity for deep internal reflection. After all, prophets carefully choose their words and every word, even if we choose to ignore them, reveals the direction we must travel so that we can be complete in Him. Each God given word in *I Kept Silence* allows Jesus to shine forth through Prophetess Omonpee and cast a shadow for our healing. She is transparent in her discourse - there is no place for satan to hide. (note — lower case)

Prophetess Omonpee develops in us, her reader, a strong desire to break out of the repressive shell of unauthorized silence and speak forth the Word of the Lord. At the same time, she teaches us to have a healthy respect for and carefully use only God given words for edification of the body of Christ. After all, it is the work of a prophet to build up and edify the body of believers. And, yes, edification sometimes tears away the old burnt and crumbling stones that are no longer fit for use. As with all prophets, the Lord reveals to them first - He revealed to Omonpee so she could teach us to become strong vessels - a sanctuary able to weather storms with a small space in the bow of the boat filled with Jesus.

- **ANITA JO MAL'AKHIM,**
Mal'akhim Ministries

Preface

Please be advised that this series of books was written by a highly anointed Prophetess of God; one with an intensely Prophetic word for a chosen Prophetic People who have a predestined Prophetic purpose. All others are certainly welcome to read this but should be advised that the revelations divulged within these pages will produce life altering aftereffects. Your thought processes will be changed. You will not be afforded the pleasure of looking at even the simplest things in life in the same way ever again. Your spiritual senses will be heightened, causing you to experience unusual sensations at the mere mention of the Prophetic. You will also experience seemingly unquenchable cravings for the deeper revelations of the Word of God. I tell you right now that, as author, I will not be held responsible for the aftermath that is sure to ensue after you read this powerful book...nor will I take credit for it. For, in Hebrews 4:12, the Bible declares the following:

"...the word of God is quick, and powerful, and sharper than any two-edged sword, piercing even to the dividing asunder of soul and spirit, and of the joints and marrow, and is a discerner of the thoughts and intents of the heart."

And, again in **Isaiah 55:11**:
"So shall my word be that goeth forth out of my mouth: it shall not return unto me void, but shall accomplish that which I please, and it shall prosper in the thing whereto I sent it."

Once we've been exposed to the true and unadulterated Word of God, as one of my favorite TV quotes states, "resistance is futile."

Prophetic People – prepare to be challenged, enlightened and enhanced. **All Others** – You're welcome to continue;

you've been duly informed of the consequences.

Formalities aside, the *"Roaring All The Day Long"* series (or *"Roaring"* series) is a microscopic view of **Psalm 32:3** and explores the silencing or constraint of a gift or calling. The source scripture – Psalm 32:3 – states the following:

"When I kept silence, my bones waxed old through my roaring all the day long."

This series offers comprehensive spiritual insight and revelatory intricacies surrounding some causes of spiritual repression, frustration and stagnation, – particularly in the lives of prophetic people. This book – *When* – is the first book in the *Roaring* series is based on the first word of Psalm 32:3. It identifies various spiritual seasons (*whens*) and gives insight as to who and when to move within and glean from these seasons, thereby causing the Divine Purpose for our lives to come into fruition.

To this point, I have given a general overview of the series. I will now give a more specific description of that this series entails. But, because of the intensely prophetic nature of the material, it is difficult to explain specifically what this series addresses without first explaining what it does not.

Psalm 32:3 was written by David after his affair with Bathsheba. The story of David and Bathsheba is a familiar one in which David, smitten with Bathsheba, arranges for her husband to be sent to the front line of battle, where he is killed. Traditionally, when this story is taught, it is always taught along the premise that David – a man after God's own heart – committed adultery and had a man killed; but then David repented. The fact that someone of David's spiritual stature could commit acts of sin and fall short of the glory of God serves as a reminder for each of us to be mindful of our spiritual state *("Wherefore let him that thinketh he standeth take heed lest he fall."* - **I Corinthians 10:12**). The concept of being spiritually aware is certainly important but **is not** the focus of the series.

The fact that David was a man after God's own heart is often skimmed over. Having a heart after God meant that David desired nothing more than to do the things that were pleasing and edifying to God. He delighted in praising and worshipping God. David loved God with his whole heart, so much so that later in the scriptures, the Bible says that David danced before the Lord so mightily until his clothes fell off **(II Samuel 6:14**). David stands as a paragon of love and adoration for God; the paradigm of a true worshipper and praiser. However, David's praise and worship **are not** the focus of this series.

How traumatic it must have been for David, who had been so intimate with God, communing with Him daily, to have committed an act of sin. It was one of which he was so ashamed, he would not share it with anyone, especially with God (i.e., *"When I* **kept silence...**"). He kept it inside and did not divulge it until such time as God sent the prophet Nathan to David with a Word that convicted him of his wrongdoing (**II Samuel 12:1-14**). David experienced deep conviction as a result of his sin. Nevertheless, David's conviction **is not** the topic of this series.

Even with a great man of God such as David, the Bible declares that it is sin that separates us from God (**Isaiah 59:2**). David, who had been anointed to serve as King of Israel; David, who loved God with all his heart and soul; David, a man after God's own heart – found himself in a place where he could no longer feel the presence of God in the same way. In this place, the anointing that had been bestowed upon him was still present, but did not flow as freely or with as much ease – his sin had produced a *spiritual constriction.* Consequently, the sin, when held in and not released **("When I kept silence")** began to penetrate his very being, causing deterioration of his spiritual foundation. That is to say, he would pray but could not hear from God. He would worship and praise but could not enter into God's presence. His foundation **("[his] bones")** became corrupt and he experienced a spiritual "osteoporosis"; i.e., **"[his] bones waxed old"**. The act of "holding it in"; the not releasing what was inside of him caused extreme frustration, lack of spiritual intimacy with God, and had he not released it, would have ultimately resulted in his spiritual death. But, God allowed David to feel an excruciating discomfort and would not allow him to become complacent in his unrepentant condition. Instead, God allowed David to enter into a spiritual state where his inner being warred within itself (another example of similar warring can be seen in **James 4:1**). This state of warring became so intense that it took on a personification, even having a "voice". The "voice" was so loud until David perceived it as a "**roaring**"; a roaring that was constant and unrelenting; a "**roaring all the day long**". This "**roaring**" – *the intense struggle and process to release what is inside of us – particularly prophetic gifts, ministries and impartations* – **is the focus of this series**.

What has God placed inside of **you** that is roaring to come forth? And why haven't you **released** it? There are many reasons why we suppress the things of the Lord and allow the *roaring* to begin in the first place. Personally, this series was birthed out of my *roaring*. The spirits of rejection and persecution, the lack of prophetic mentorship and other factors contributed to the *roaring* in my life.

For years, I went through spiritual repression and frustration, afraid to be who God called me to be. I was afraid of the reactions of those around me. I was called of God as early as 5 years old but was not ordained as a minister until I was 15. Even as a teenager, I knew beyond a shadow of a doubt that God had a great calling upon my life. Wanting to "fit in" with the crowd, but never really being able to do so, I suppressed the gift of the Prophetic and the calling to the office of the Prophet. I hoped and prayed that someone – *anyone* would accept and appreciate me.

Yes, God would bless me to have moments of release; I would minister a Prophetic Word here or sing praises there. Nevertheless, each time, the enemy would make sure that my same old nemeses —Rejection and Persecution — would be right there to torment me. They would come namely in the form of "Church Folk", who had neither an understanding of nor a calling to the Prophetic. It became a vicious cycle that eventually wore me out. Not having the strength to fight anymore, I stopped trying. As I became an adult, the Lord blessed me to find a place — LoveJoy Outreach Ministries in Metropolis, Illinois — in which I was taught the "basics" about Divine revelation. However, the Lord had even more in store for me.

The Lord blessed me to get married to a wonderful Christian man and move to Texas, still hurt and bruised from childhood scars. However, I found the same spirits of rejection and persecution running rampant in the churches in that particular area. Disappointed and tired of trying, I retreated into my own little world for a span of about five years. I still had a relationship with God; I still received Prophetic revelations but was not willing to fellowship with any one body of Believers (in my mind, *Me + Church Folk = Hurt*). Nor did I want to share what I received from the Lord with anyone, for fear of being rejected or ridiculed. I had a singular goal in mind: I did not want to preach or, for that matter, hear anyone else preach. I did not want to prophesy. I certainly did not want to write a book. **My goal**, I concluded, **was simply to be left alone**. And, as for my goal, I would have achieved it, too.... **had it not been for that confounded roaring**!

The *roaring* was the thing that kept me awake all night, pondering the things of the Lord, although my flesh did not want to do so. It was the force that kept driving me and would not let me be complacent, although I purposed in my heart not to go one step further in ministry. The *roaring* was the thing that would not let me commit suicide, even at my lowest point because somewhere deep inside me I knew that there was great ministry and enormous worth. It was the gnawing and pulling in my spirit toward revelatory teachings and messages. The *roaring* was the unquenchable desire to fulfill God's Divine Purpose for my life; unquenchable because nothing else would fill the void. Nothing else would make me happy or give me peace. **Nothing short of fulfilling God's Divine Purpose for my life would stop the roaring.**

So, through a series of events (some to which I will refer throughout the series), I made up my mind to stop the *roaring*. I began to actively seek to do God's Will and fulfill His Divine Purpose for my life. The *roaring* has subsided because the ministry, which was once trapped within me, is now freely flowing out of me and into the lives of other Believers. My "**bones**", though they still ache from years of neglect, are no longer "**waxing old**"; I am now free.

In Luke **22:32**, the Bible says, *"...and when thou are converted, strengthen thy brethren";* writing this series of books is my first step toward doing just that.

With each word that I write, I am silencing the *roaring* in my spirit. I am being taken to another level in God, one in which Prophetic revelation is increased and the promises of God are made manifest. It is a place of awesome power; a place of infinite joy; a place of unending spiritual growth *("from glory to glory").* Come – *Prophetic People and All Others* – and go with me to that place through the pages of these books.

Introduction
Deadly Silence

As I am penning these words, I am honored, excited and relieved to be able to embark upon this book – ***I Kept Silence*** – the second book in the ***Roaring All the Day Long*** series. Firstly, I am *honored* because once again, God has seen fit to bless me to be able to teach His people via the ministry of prophetic writing that He has given me. Secondly, I am *excited* because even I am not 100 percent sure what the Lord will say or do in the writing of this book, but I feel in my spirit that God will allow us to discover even more profound prophetic revelation than in ***When***, the first book in the ***Roaring*** series. Lastly, I am *relieved*. This book has been a work in the makings for approximately nine years! Many things have happened that have interfered with me completing this work, but, praise be to God that His Word "*shall not return unto [Him] void, but it shall accomplish that which I please, and it shall prosper in the thing where to [He] sent it* (Isaiah 55:11). God gave me the mandate to write this series and, whether now or nine years ago, and, no matter what things happened or events transpired to prevent me from writing, this book MUST be written and come to pass, for the Glory of God and the building of the prophetic people in the earth realm.

Among the things that have happened since the publication of ***When*** is the death of my friend Edwina Allen. Readers will recall that Edwina wrote the Foreword for ***When***. What readers may or may not know is that Sis. Edwina was also prophetic friend mentioned in the Introduction of ***When***. I am ever cognizant of the impact that she has had on both my life and my ministry. As I type this portion with tears in my eyes, I miss Edwina greatly, but am comforted by my sincere belief that she is now in a better place, no longer in pain or turmoil, but now is resting with God for eternity.

Another of things that has prohibited me from writing this book sooner is simply life itself. Although I will not go into long, drawn-out details, since the writing of the first book, I have been through much spiritual warfare and even warfare against my health. Particularly, I had been diagnosed with thyroid cancer, had a thyroidectomy and, praise God, now have a clean bill of health. I have been shaken – nearly to the core – by events in my life that, admittedly, have at times caused me to question my level of commitment and purpose. I wondered if I had the "right" (and, at times, admittedly, did not have the desire) to prophesy, teach, or write. I have suffered spiritual attack on my mind, resulting in suppression, oppression and depression. I wanted to do nothing but cry and had feelings of deep depression and isolation. In fact, this warfare…these life events…had temporarily ***silenced*** me. That is, this warfare had prevented me from *saying or doing that which God had commanded me to do.*

But, praises be to God, who *"will not leave us comfortless"* (John 14:18). Even with the absence of my prophetic friend who inspired me in the writing of the first book, God yet sent someone to minister to me in my time of need and deliver a life-changing Word that set me free and caused me to continue on my course. In fact, there were two elders who God used to speak to me. One of these ministers told me, "God is NOT going to change His mind; you must still do what God told you to do in the first place." The second elder delivered a powerful word in which he told me that, whatever I was dealing with would have to be left at the altar THAT day (*"…To day if ye will hear his voice, harden not your heart…"*[Psalms 95:7b and 8a]). I will be eternally grateful to these two men of God, who ministered the much-needed, well-timed Word of God to me in this season.

And, if indeed our misery is our ministry, then it makes sense to me that, out of this heart-wrenching time of my life, God would have me to draw and glean for the framework for this book. During this time, I began to see more clearly how we can be silenced and the many reasons we do not allow that which God has placed inside of us to come forth; I do not have to ***prophesy*** it, but can now ***testify*** it because, even if only for a relatively short period of time I ***walked*** it; I ***felt*** it; I ***lived*** it. (*"...[I] speak that that [I] do know, and testify that [I] have seen"* [John 3:11b]).

During that time of silence, God began to deal with me even more about silence itself. He showed me how I—a prophet who professes to walk closely with God, speaking His mysteries to His people and communing with Him on a continuous basis—could fall prey to the trick of the enemy to keep even the prophet silent. How much more then, He said, could others also be affected by these tricks of the enemy; tactics to keep the Body of Christ from growing and flowing in the things of God; tactics that cut them off (*"...insomuch that, if [it were] possible, they shall deceive the very elect."* [Matthew 24:24d])? Whatever the source of the silence (that is, whatever keeps people from not expressing the God in themselves and doing what God has told them to do), the end result planned by the enemy was **death** - spiritual and, oftentimes, physical as well.

God then showed how ***deadly*** the silence itself is. He said that while silence can sometimes be good and is sometimes required (*"Be silent, O all flesh, before the LORD: for he is raised up out of his holy habitation* [Zechariah 2:13]). However, that is **not** the type of silence that we will be exploring in this book. Instead, we will be exploring the type of prolonged, "unauthorized", deadly silence that

David experienced in the source scripture for the Roaring series, Psalms 32:3. In it, David, a man after God's own heart, was lamenting what had happened to him because of his disobedience and disconnection from God. He was saying that his keeping silence felt likened unto his very bones waxing old - a *spiritual osteoporosis* (that we will discuss in the Conclusion of this book and in ***My Bones Waxed Old***, the third book in the ***Roaring*** series) - that, if left unattended, could have eventually killed him.

There is a paralysis, God says, which takes place, which causes a prophetic rigor mortis to set in as spiritual death takes over. The person in whom this happens is unaware of it at first, but in time becomes paralyzed, so to speak. Because the person has either refused to flow in his or her calling or has been hindered from doing so in some way, he or she cannot move in God like they once did. They try to speak or do, but, because the muscles have not been used in such a long time, they are unable to act or act much slowly or with not as much accuracy as they once did.

God said that a person in this state is a "sitting duck" for an attack of the enemy. When a prophetic person is in such a state, they are not only endangered, but become a danger to others in the Body of Christ because they can no longer be depended upon to "pull their weight" in terms of ministry and therefore leave the other parts of the Body exposed and in need of whatever ministry the "missing in action" part would have provided (*"From whom the whole body fitly joined together and compacted by that which every joint supplieth, according to the effectual working in the measure of every part, maketh increase of the body unto the edifying of itself in love"* [Ephesians 4:16]).

Again, from my personal experience, during my time of silence, I can recall being so paralyzed with depression and self-doubt until I would not move. I did not want to hear

God, nor did I want to prophesy. I just wanted to be left alone. But, in my wanting to be left alone, I was shutting out both God and the people of God to whom I was connected and obligated to minister to and with whom I am commanded by the Word to fellowship (i.e., *"Am I my brother's keeper*?[Genesis 4:9c]). Souls and lives placed in my spiritual care were being neglected by my silence, and, God said, so are the lives of many, whose spiritual leaders, mentors and overseers have been silenced. To illustrate this to me, God gave me the following sets of scriptures.

Isaiah 61:1-3 declares the following:

> *The Spirit of the Lord God is upon me; because the Lord hath anointed me to* ***preach*** *good tidings unto the meek; he hath sent me to* ***bind up*** *the brokenhearted, to* ***proclaim*** *liberty to the captives, and the* ***opening of the prison*** *to them that are bound.*
>
> *To* ***proclaim*** *the acceptable year of the Lord, and the vengeance of our God; to* ***comfort*** *all that mourn;*
>
> *To* ***appoint*** *unto them that mourn in Zion, to give unto them beauty for ashes, the oil of joy for mourning, the garment of praise for the spirit of heaviness; that they might be called trees of righteousness, the planting of the Lord, that he might be glorified.*

And, Romans 10:14-18 says:

> *For whosoever shall* ***call*** *upon the name of the Lord shall be saved.*
>
> *How then shall they* ***call*** *on him in whom they have not* ***believed****? And how shall they* ***believe*** *in him of whom*

> *they have not **heard**? And how shall they **hear** without a **preacher**?*
>
> *And how shall they **preach**, except they be **sent**? as it written, How beautiful are the feet of them that preach the gospel of peace, and bring glad tidings of good things!*
>
> *But they have not all obeyed the gospel. For Esaias saith, Lord, who hath believed our report?*
>
> *So then **faith** cometh by **hearing**, and **hearing** by the word of God.*
>
> *But I say, Have they not **heard**? Yes verily, their **sound** went into all the earth, and their words unto the ends of the world.*

Finally, Romans 10:8-10 says this:

> *But what saith it? The **word** is nigh thee, **even in thy mouth**, and in thy heart: that is, the **word of faith**, which we **preach**;*
>
> *That if thou shalt **confess** with thy mouth the Lord Jesus, and shalt believe in thine heart that God hath raised him from the dead, thou shalt be saved.*
>
> *For with the heart man believeth unto righteousness; and with the **mouth confession is made unto salvation.***

Remember that our definition of silence is *the act of not doing or saying what God has given you/ordained you to do.* So, then, when we read the above scriptures found in Isaiah 61, we see then that the God has sent His Spirit and His Anointing for the express purpose of enabling and empowering us to ***say*** (*preach, proclaim*) and ***do*** *(bind up, opening of prison, comfort, appoint, give)*.

After God showed me this, He then said, "So, if there were no ***preaching***, what would happen to the meek?" And, "If there were no ***binding up***, what would happen to the brokenhearted? What would happen to the captives, if there were no ***proclaiming*** and what about the bound, if there were no ***opening of the prison***? What would become of those who mourn, if there were no one to ***comfort*** them?"

God then showed me that the very crux of salvation is based on the idea of not keeping silent. Regarding the Romans 10 scriptures, God said to me, "If I [God] ***kept silent***, the preacher would not hear. And, if the preacher did not hear, he could not ***preach*** salvation to the people. And, if the preacher kept silent and could not preach salvation to the people, then the people would not ***believe*** because they would not have ***heard*** the message. If the people did not believe, then they would not ***call*** upon Me and ***confess***, in order to be saved."

And, of course, while the gift of God is eternal life as a result of salvation, no salvation in Jesus Christ results in spiritual death and eternal damnation (*"For the wages of sin is death; but the gift of God is eternal life through Jesus Christ our Lord"* [Romans 6:23]*)*.

Silence, then, in this sense, becomes ***deadly***. It produces death in our present lives in that we live beneath our prophetic privilege. We are then shortchanging others and ourselves of the many wonderful gifts and callings that God has placed inside of us. It can also produce spiritual death and possible eternal damnation. We must be sure that we are not keeping this type of silence for too long, as it is not the Will of God for our lives.

That being said, I must again reference the second of the two Elders who prayed for me during my time of silence. In addition to telling me what God said about the silence ending "that day", he also prophesied that God told him that I was 10 years behind schedule with the things of the Lord in my life!!! But, he said, God would allow me to "catch up" in a span of 36 months! Praise be to God for grace and mercy to allow me to catch up and to complete that which He has assigned to my hands. It is with that Word from the Lord that I repented for my prolonged and "unauthorized" silence and steadfastly began to seek Him regarding the writing of this book and the completion of the ***Roaring*** series. And, as I sought Him, He gave me what I am now giving to you in the pages of this book.

The primary chapters of this book will be titled with a word or a phrase whose first letter is a corresponding letter in the word **SILENT**. Each of these chapters will expound upon a word or phrase which could be a cause of one not fulfilling his or her prophetic purpose and doing what God has called them to do.

The last section of this book is the Conclusion, entitled, "*Silence of the Limbs*", which God actually gave me when the writing of ***When*** was completed. It is both a teaching and prophetic utterance regarding His Body and its "limbs" and why we - The Trees of Righteousness - are not fully functioning in the earth realm. This will serve as the end of this book - which discusses what causes the silence - and will lead into ***My Bones Waxed Old*** - which will describe the aftermath of the silencing.

Many of the base scriptures for these chapters were taken from a list of scriptures that I read during my time of silence. As I read these scriptures and began the process of being set free from my silence, I found these scriptures to bring new life into my spirit. Likewise, it is my prayer for the readers that the words on these pages will be rhema to you and will speak life into any dead areas; I believe God that this work will "silence your silencers" and do for me what the word from the Elder did: *provoke you to be about your Father's business with haste and zeal.*

S

Scared

During my prayer time, I sought answers as to what this chapter was to be about. I felt the Lord leading me to examine my own prolonged period of silence for the answer. I came up with encountering the swine spirit (again, another chapter for another time), but I also felt that rejection and a few other strongholds were factors in my being silenced. God showed me that, yes, these were things that the enemy used against me to keep me from not going forward with my purpose. But, He showed me that they were **not** the main culprits. He said that there was something larger, deeper, more sinister in the background that enabled the rejection and swine spirits to have the intended negative impact in my life.

Then, the Lord showed me a gun. Rather, He showed someone loading bullets into the chamber of a gun. As the person was loading the gun, I could see words written on the sides of the bullets: **REJECTION** and some others. At that point, I began to understand what the Lord was saying. Yes, the "bullets" were doing the damage, but what was ***propelling*** them toward me with deadly force? Not, "***who***", because we know that that was the enemy (for the Bible says "*The thief cometh not, but for to steal, and to kill, and to destroy...*" [John 10:10a]). But, the question was, "***What*** was the 'gun'?" ***What*** set in motion these destructive forces that kept penetrating my mind, seemingly puncturing my spirit, with intent to bring my spiritual demise?

I began to think about the times that I had experienced rejection and how it made me feel. I began to examine ***why*** it was an issue. Since the writing of *When,* I have grown by leaps and bounds in my walk with the Lord. Rejection does not affect me the same way that it used to – Praise Him! So, I had to press in and find out what the problem ***used to be***. At that point, I had the following conversation with myself:

Okay, so that person rejected me. How did that used to make me feel (before I was delivered from rejection)?
Badly.
How does it make me feel now?
I honestly don't care.
WHY don't I care?
Because there is nothing that that person's accepting or rejecting me can do to me or for me.
Okay, then why did I care in the first place?
Because I thought I NEEDED them to accept me, until I couldn't get them to and found out I didn't.

Aha!

And, if I thought that I ***needed*** the person's acceptance, then the thought of not having it made me feel uncomfortable. So, then, the real problem was not necessarily that I was being **rejected**; the root of the problem was that I had a **fear** of not being accepted, which gave place to the spirit of rejection. I was ***scared***!

This chapter will explore the role that ***fear*** – being ***scared*** – plays in the silencing of a gift or calling. It will also discuss different types of fears and manifestations – telltale signs – of fear in the life of the Believer. Once we can recognize the signs, we can take measures to eradicate fear from our lives, to keep it from stifling our spiritual growth and hindering our walk.

WHAT IS FEAR?

In order to talk about being scared, we must first understand fear. According to the New Oxford American Dictionary, the most common definition for fear is defined as, *"an unpleasant emotion caused by the belief that someone or something is dangerous, likely to cause pain or a threat."*

It is, then, the belief that something is going to cause pain that triggers the unpleasant emotion of fear. What we **believe** plays a role in what we are afraid of or what scares us. Therefore, what we don't believe plays a role in what we are not afraid of or what does not scare us. The Bible decrees that, *"For as he thinketh in his heart, so is he..."* (Proverbs 23:7). Therefore, whatever a person *thinks* or *believes* will dictate his actions, his philosophy about life, and his fears.

For instance, if a person is afraid of snakes, then that person believes that snakes are dangerous and are likely to cause them pain and is threatened by snakes. But, if a person is not afraid of snakes, then that person does not believe that snakes are dangerous and are not likely to cause the person pain. The person does not ***perceive*** snakes to be a threat.

So, then, fear boils down to ***what we believe*** and ***what we don't believe***. As Believers, we are supposed to ***believe*** in the Word of God and His Promises - both those in the Bible and those He has spoken to our spirit. In short, Believers are supposed to ***believe*** what God says is true and are ***not supposed to believe*** that what the enemy says is true.

This belief in God and His Word is called ***faith in God***. When we have faith in God, we do not have faith in what the enemy says and we close all portals through which he can speak to us. The belief in anything or anyone who does not say what God says about a situation is called ***doubt and/or unbelief***. When we do not have faith in God, we are actually operating in ***faith in the enemy***. There is no middle ground.

Prophet Essien Godwin, senior pastor of Reigners' Palace (Church) and founder of Global Prophetic and Healing Outreach International in Kumasi, Ghana, best explained it this way:

> *Faith comes by hearing and hearing the word of GOD (Romans 10:17). Doubt, unbelief, and fear come by choosing to hear the whispering of the devil and the senses.*

Fear vs. Faith

Faith, then, ***is the absence of fear***. ***Fear***, then, ***is the absence of faith***. With faith, we can do anything the Lord requires of us. And, in the absence of faith, we cannot do anything for the Lord. We cannot walk out our calling or purpose. In the absence of faith, we are silenced. This is because the Word of God declares the following:

> *But without faith it is impossible to please him: for he that cometh to God must believe that he is, and that he is a rewarder of them that diligently seek him.*– **Hebrews 11:6**

And, again:

> *Now the just shall live by faith: but if any man draw back, my soul shall have no pleasure in him.*
>
> *But we are not of them who draw back unto perdition; but of them that believe to the saving of the soul.*
>
> – **Hebrews 10:38-39**

WHAT IS FAITH?

Because this chapter is about being scared and the negative consequences that come with it, I do not intend to study faith extensively in this chapter. I would, however, be remiss in any discussion of faith by not giving at least a base definition of it and expounding upon the purpose of faith in the life of the Believer. I will also show how faith is the antithesis of being scared (or, fear).

No discussion of faith in God would be complete without an exegesis of Hebrews 11, which is also known as the Faith chapter. Hebrews 11:1 gives us a succinct yet powerful description of faith, and reads as follows:

> *Now faith is the substance of things hoped for, the evidence of things not seen.*

So, from this verse, we see that faith is considered both a *substance* and *evidence*. God showed me that, in our physical world, both ***substances*** and ***evidence*** are tangible and/or "concrete". That is, both ***substances*** and ***evidence*** can be measured by some quantitative standard. There is a way of viewing the "amount" or "deficit" of them. They are the "elements" that comprise the "things hoped for" and the "things not seen". God showed me that the characteristics of faith being both a ***substance*** and ***evidence*** are key in understanding what faith is, how it works, and why faith is the absence of fear.

Faith in Action

The Lord then told me to research the definition of ***evidence***. I thought I knew what this meant, but in obedience I researched the definition. Evidence means, *"the available body of facts or information indicating whether a belief or proposition is true or valid"*. So, then, ***evidence*** means **proof**.

Revisiting the Faith chapter - Hebrews 11 - we see many examples the ***evidence***, i.e., **proof**, of faith. I have cited verses 2 through 5 below. Please note that the evidence (listed in ***bold italics***) is the **result** of the faith.

> *For by it* (faith) *the elders **obtained** a good report.*
>
> *Through **faith** we **understand** that the worlds were framed by the word of God, so that things which are seen were not made of things which do appear.*
>
> *By **faith** Abel **offered** unto God a more excellent sacrifice than Cain, by which he **obtained** witness that he was righteous, God testifying of his gifts: and by it he being dead yet speaketh.*
>
> *By **faith** Enoch **was translated** that he should not see death; and was not found, because God had translated him: for before his translation he had this testimony, that he pleased God.*

Each example of ***evidence*** shown above is a verb. Verbs are parts of speech that show action. So, then we see that each evidence is in reality an action set into motion or brought to past as a result of faith. In verse two, by faith, the elders obtained a good report. Through faith (in verse 3) we understand that the worlds were framed by the word of God. And so it continues for most of Hebrews 11. We see, then, that ***faith yields action. Lack of faith,* then, *yields a lack of action.***

Substantial Evidence

Then, the Lord then directed me to look up the meaning of the word, ***substance***, because the scripture says that faith is the substance of things hoped for. In fact, the word substance began to repeat in my spirit. When the Lord directed me to do this, I felt a leaping in my spirit as if He were going to reveal something profound to me, but I did not know what just yet.

Three definitions of ***substance*** are as follows:

1. *a particular kind of matter with uniform properties*
2. *the real physical matter of which a person or thing consists and which has a tangible, solid presence*
    - *the quality of having a solid basis in reality or fact*
    - *the quality of being dependable or*
3. *the quality of being important, valid, or significant*
    - *the most important or essential part of something; the real or essential meaning*

While I understood this definition, I didn't immediately grasp the fullness of the revelation that God wanted me to glean from it. Then, I was meditating on all of this while taking a break from writing this chapter (God deals with each person differently. With me, when I am writing, I write a while, then I get up and walk around taking a break but listening to Him and hearing what to write next.). At that point, God gave me a revelation concerning **hormones**! He showed me in a vision the definition of hormones. I had never looked up the definition of hormones before, but I knew instantly what He said showed me was right, because God is not a man that He should lie (Numbers 23:19). Then, He instantly "confirmed" what He was telling me. He gave me ***evidence*** that what He was saying is correct. He told me to go and look up the definition of *hormone.*

The definition of hormone as follows:

> *"A regulatory* ***substance*** *produced in an organism and transported in tissue fluids such as blood or sap to stimulate specific cells or tissues into action; a synthetic substance with a similar effect."*

When I read this, my spirit leapt! God does indeed use the foolish things of the world to confound the wise (I Corinthians 1:27)! I laughed! It instantly became rhema to me. Here is why:

While writing this chapter, I am a one-year diagnosed thyroid cancer survivor. In May of 2009, I was diagnosed - rather unexpectedly I might add - with papillary carcinoma, the slowest spreading form of thyroid cancer. The next month - June - I had my thyroid removed. I am thanking God for being as healthy as I am and am believing God for total victory and healing, for the Word decrees that *"By His stripes ye are healed"* (I Peter 12:24e) and, *"Healing is the children's bread"* (Matthew 15:26). But, with the thyroid gone, the hormones that it made that are essential to life and various functions in the body were gone, too. Because of spiritual warfare via bad healthcare, I underwent an egregious period in which the doctor did not prescribe hormones and delayed treatment. God kept me! My tests showed that my TSH (thyroid stimulating hormone; produced by the pituitary gland when your thyroid is not making enough hormones) was at stroke levels. But, God brought me through.

Things that I have done all my life - breathing, sleeping, walking, typing, eating, thinking, writing and moving, just to name a few - were all affected by the lack of hormones. My muscles locked up and my body seemed to want to freeze in a fetal position. My fingers were swollen and sore, so that I could almost not type, let alone write. And, even if I would want to write, my ability to focus, to spell even the simplest of words, to remember what I was writing - all of that was affected because of hormones. My knees hurt so much until I sometimes could not bear to walk. I was in pain constantly. My sleep patterns were altered and I experienced vivid, realistic nightmares. My quality of life diminished greatly. I found myself not wanting to move, to write, to do anything. My moods were altered greatly. Had it continued, it would have meant my certain death.

I prayed and God moved. I was blessed with a new doctor who had my best interests at heart. He immediately performed the radioactive iodine (RAI) treatment to kill any errant thyroid cells and then put me on hormones. It has been a challenge to regulate the hormones, but it is necessary. One hormone pill daily is what I take. Hormone pills have become a huge part of my life. But, the hormones I take are not from a human's body; they are synthetic and called hormone replacement therapy (HRT).

So, then, when God gave me this revelation on the definition of hormone — *a regulatory* ***substance*** *produced in an organism and transported in tissue fluids such as blood or sap to* ***stimulate*** *specific cells or tissues* ***into action*** - it just all made sense! Both faith and hormones are **substances** that cause or **enable action**! Just like without hormones my body couldn't function....

> *"...**without faith** it is **impossible to please him**: for he that cometh to God must believe that he is, and that he is a rewarder of them that diligently seek him. "*
>
> **– Hebrews 11:6**

With my having just experienced severe hormone deficiency and a plethora of associated side effects, this revelation was golden to me! I could now see so clearly why the Body of Christ is not where it should be and why it is functioning at a fraction of the amount of power and authority it should be demonstrating. God has called us to rise up and walk in our authority in the earth realm; the Word declares that we are the head and not the tail (Deuteronomy 28:13); the lenders and not the borrowers (Deuteronomy 15:6). The Word also tells us that we are blessed in the city and blessed in the field (Deuteronomy 28:3). Jesus Himself said that while He did miracles, that the works that He did, we as Believers would do those and greater (John 14:12). And yet, we do not see the fruits described in the scriptures manifesting in our lives. God showed me that a primary reason for this is ***a lack of faith,*** which means ***an abundance of fear.***

A "Hormoneous" Revelation

God said our spiritual hormones are off! And we are seeing the manifestations of this spiritual malady being brought forth in the physical realm! Do we have a Body (of Christ)? Yes! Does the body have parts sufficient for it to function properly (I Corinthians 12:27)? Yes. Do we have blood (salvation [I John 1:7])? Yes. Do we have food to eat and water to drink (the Word of God, both bread and meat [Hebrews 5:12])? Yes. But, the parts are not functioning to their fullest potential and for the express purpose for which God made them. Just as in the physical body with its hormones, when *faith* - **our spiritual hormones** - is not where they should be, there are various and sundry issues with the Body.

God also showed me that our spiritual hormones - *faith* - are not stable. He said that we are not always consistent with what we Believe, allowing fear, doubt and unbelief to creep in and cause our faith level to decrease. When this happens, we become double-minded. The Bible says that "a double-minded" man is unstable in all his ways (James 1:8). In the physical realm, a person with severe hormone fluctuations experiences dizziness, personality changes, mood swings - they become "unstable, in all their ways". Likewise, in the spirit realm, when our faith waivers, we are "wishy-washy" and do not walk in our vocation and/or calling with the consistency, accuracy and passion that we once did.

Have your dreams for yourself and your future changed for the worse? Have you experienced spiritual "hair loss" (i.e., loss of strength, like Samson [Judges 16:19])? Or, do you have excessive hair growth in unwanted areas, making you "unsightly" and unpleasant to look at (Dan. 4:33)? Does it hurt when you try to "walk"? Do your spiritual knees hurt; is it painful for you to pray? Are you finding it difficult to concentrate on what you are supposed to be doing because of negative distractions around you/in your life? Do you have an inexplicable sense of dread and foreboding that has caused your attitude to change so that you are now pessimistic? Do you cry at the drop of a hat? Does it seem that you have lost your motivation, focus and/or purpose? If you answered, "Yes" to any of these questions, God said to check your **spiritual hormone levels** - ***your faith level***. When our faith level is where it is supposed to be, we are up and at 'em and are ready, willing and able to walk out our prophetic destiny and calling. When our faith level is not where it should be, we become vulnerable to the tricks of the enemy, whose purpose is to keep us from completing our assignments here on earth. This is because when we are not operating at a sufficient faith level, we are open to fear in its many forms.

TYPES OF FEAR

Revisiting the definition of fear, we remember that fear is, "*an unpleasant emotion caused by the belief that someone or something is dangerous, likely to cause pain or a threat.*" We see that our fear of something is predicated on our belief that something or someone will cause us pain or be a threat to us in some way and/or that something or someone is dangerous. In order to understand fear, we must first understand pain. Pain is defined as:

> *"physical suffering or discomfort caused by illness or injury; a feeling of marked discomfort in a particular part of the body ;mental suffering or distress".*

Pain comes in several forms, and can be physical, mental, spiritual or emotional. And, because there are different types of pain, there are also several different types of fear. However, for purposes of this chapter, I will draw from my personal experiences and discuss two common types of fears with which I have struggled - ***the fear of rejection and the fear of failure.***

Fear of Rejection

The first type of fear that we will discuss will be the fear of rejection. Specifically, this is a fear of being rejected by an individual or group. To be rejected means to be, "*dismissed as inadequate, inappropriate, or not to one's taste.*" When someone rejects you, they have, "*failed to show due affection or concern for (someone)*" or they have "*rebuffed*" the object of the rejection. When a person is the object of rejection, the person often feels like they don't fit in, they are not "good enough", no one likes them, and, in many instances, the person **believes** this to the degree that the **belief** affects his or her self-perception, self-confidence and self-worth. The person (the Rejected) seems himself or herself through the eyes of the person or group doing the rejecting (the Rejecter).

A fear of rejection is rooted in the spirit of rejection. Rejection is an ungodly spirit that is sent from the enemy to keep us from walking out our destiny and calling. It does this in several ways, including causing the person who is being rejected to **doubt** himself or herself and his or her ability to do what God has told them to do. Rejection also hinders our walk by inflicting severe emotional pain on the person. Rejection is a gateway spirit—the door for other spirits to come in and further hinder the person from walking in his or her calling. These other spirits include but are not limited to not forgiving, an inability to trust, a spirit of being judgmental, insecurity, paranoia, hatred (of the Rejecter[s] and of self), and, in some cases, suicide.

The fear of rejection is a type of fear with which I am altogether too familiar. From a child, I remember being rejected and being alienated and persecuted. While I know now that rejection and persecution are the prerequisite to walking in the Office of a Prophet, ("*And he said, Verily I say unto you, No prophet is accepted in his own country.*" [Luke 4:24]), I did not know it growing up, nor that I was even called to the Office of the Prophet. Had I been armed with that knowledge, I may or may not have experienced the emotional and spiritual scars I received because I internalized and personalized a lot of the rejection I received. I was rejected by people in the church world, in ministry, at school, in my personal life - in every arena, I experienced rejection. But, apparently, that rejection was needed to make me into who I was destined to be.

Ridding myself of the fear of rejection has been and is an ongoing process. Part of the reason for this is I was not taught how to do so. Another reason is I had suppressed many memories of being rejected because they were painful, and I did not have the spiritual knowledge to deal with them yet.

One such incident of being rejected occurred during my late teen years and the Rejecter(s) were people in ministry. I was made to feel inadequate and left out; I was mocked and made to be the butt of jokes of other parishioners. It was only this year when I encountered these people on Facebook - after nearly 20 years of not seeing or hearing from them - did all of these feelings of rejection re-surface. I was both shocked and disappointed that I, a person who walks in her calling and who has prayed for others' deliverance from rejection, was the very one who stood in need of deliverance from rejection herself.

I prayed about this and God showed me that best way to confront this fear was to meet it head on. God instructed me to get in the Word more and to speak forgiveness out of my mouth toward these people anytime a negative or painful thought concerning them came up in my spirit. God showed me that in order to forgive them for rejecting me, I had to be willing to let go of my desire to "get even" or to "show them" (common motivations for people who have a fear of rejection). God also showed me how being rejected by them had caused the fear of rejection to take root in my spirit and to hinder me. He further showed me that all those years ago, the enemy -the father of lies (John 8:44) - had planted a seed of doubt and unbelief in me as it related to rejection.

When they re-entered my life, I began to second-guess myself in a lot of areas, because that is what they used to do me. Was my writing good enough? Who did I think I was to be writing a book anyway? I found myself monitoring my behavior based on what I thought they would or would not like, just to "show them" that I was not what they said I was or, rather, that I was more than they ever thought I would be. But, the Lord showed me that, in doing that I was really putting those people and their opinion of me in the place where God would be in my life. And, He also showed me that I was not hurting anyone but me; I was hindering myself from flowing in the fullness of God and what He had for my life. The relationship with these people was in the past and I could not effectively go forward while looking backward.

God revealed to me, though, that there is indeed a blessing in this; a proverbial silver lining in this cloud. As I called upon a group of trusted friends and confidants for counsel, prayer and encouragement during this time and bore my soul to them about this, God used these friends to show me that what the enemy meant for evil by inflicting this pain of rejection on me all those years ago has actually been a ***blessing*** to me.

God has done a great work in me and has matured me in my walk as a prophet. I am now entrusted with others who learn from me and look to me for spiritual guidance, just as I looked to the leaders who rejected me. However, the years of rejection taught me to never, ever treat people like I had treated! I am ever so careful as to how I handle a member of the Body of Christ and people in general. So, what the enemy meant for evil, God meant for good "to save much people alive" (Genesis 50:20). I am blessed to have Facebook friends and ministry contacts from all over the world. And, many of them did not believe in God or did not read their Bibles prior to meeting me. But, I have had many to tell me that because of the way I "handled" them - with compassion, respect and in love - that they have started to ***consider*** Christianity and trusting in God. I had to be a living epistle, known and read of men (I Corinthians 3:2) to get their attention and to draw them in loving-kindness (Jeremiah 31:3). I have no doubt, the painful experiences I encountered played a large part in the way I **choose** to represent God in the earth realm.

Jabez

The Biblical character of Jabez is a good example of one who has been rejected. What little we know of Jabez is found in only two verses in the Bible - I Chronicles 4:9-10. The story of Jabez is a follows:

> *And Jabez was more honourable than his brethren: and his mother called his name Jabez, saying, Because I bare him with sorrow.*
>
> *And Jabez called on the God of Israel, saying, Oh that thou wouldest bless me indeed, and enlarge my coast, and that thine hand might be with me, and that thou wouldest keep me from evil, that it may not grieve me! And God granted him that which he requested.*

In verse 9, we find that Jabez's name means, "*I bare him with sorrow*". So, from Jabez's birth, he was thought of as a source of pain for his mother. In Biblical days, the meanings of names were taken more seriously than perhaps they are today. So, then, whenever anyone called Jabez (i.e., said his name), they were saying that his coming into the world was a source of sorrow for his mother. This would have been considered a "scourge" upon him. He would have, in all probability, been looked upon with disdain. He would have been "*dismissed as inadequate, inappropriate, or not to one's taste.*" More than likely, people in his community "*failed to show due affection or concern for him"*; they would have *"rebuffed"* Jabez. Jabez, more than likely, was ***rejected***!

We can only imagine what type of life Jabez had. The Bible does not speak of his childhood; it does not tell of his journey through rejection. We do not get to read of his highs and lows, nor do we ever really know what caused his mother to name him as she did. The Bible says, *"All scripture [is] given by inspiration of God, and [is] profitable for doctrine, for reproof, for correction, for instruction in righteousness: That the man of God may be perfect, throughly furnished unto all good works."* (II Timothy 3:16-17). So, then, perhaps God did not consider it "profitable" for us to know Jabez's struggle. But, what He did reveal through scripture is this: Jabez prayed and God granted his request!

God said to tell you that, as He did with Jabez' rejection, He will use your story of rejection to minister to others.

Fear of Failure

The fear of failure is another common fear, both with Believers and non-Believers. In preparing to write this portion of this chapter, I came across many articles that dealt with failure/failing God in terms of sin and iniquity. While it is true that we fail God when we go against His Word, that particular type of failure is not that to which I am referring. In fact, failing God through sin will be discussed in *Chapter L: Little Foxes.* Instead, for purposes of this discussion, fear of failure is simply this: *being apprehensive about doing what God has told/called/instructed/ordained you to do because you are afraid that you will not be successful in your execution or completion of the assignment.*

Some people live all their lives in fear of failure and never even attempt to fulfill their destiny. And, some start doing what God has told them to do, but then they allow the fear of failure to set in and begin to have doubt. In their minds, they don't doubt that God can do it; instead ***they are deceived into doubting that they can do what God told them to do.*** The fear of failure is a bondage that is sent straight from the pits of hell. It is oppressive and causes the person to become frustrated.

I know from personal experience that the fear of failure is stifling, incapacitating, and takes one to a very dark place. For me, the fear of failure would always attack when I am in the bed, trying to sleep; I am not sure why except that perhaps when we are sleeping we are the most vulnerable (as Samuel found out in I Samuel 3:4 when God spoke to him in his sleep). Nevertheless, the fear of failure would come and I would start to have thoughts of doom and gloom. I have literally felt fear "grip my heart" (I know now that that was anxiety and possibly a mild panic attack). Then, the negative thoughts would set in. "I have wasted my life", I would think. "I am not where I wanted to be at this point in my life. **Why** did my life turn out this way? Am I *ever* going to be the person I saw myself being? What is going to happen to me in the future? Maybe it would just be best if I died right now." I would hear these thoughts repeatedly. They were torturous. Before long, a heaviness would set in and I would find myself crying.

Then, whatever I was working on at that time in my life seemed to become either more difficult to complete and unimportant/insignificant. At the same time, feelings of anxiety, helplessness and hopelessness would surface. Before long, I would become overwhelmed and not able to concentrate on the task or assignment at hand. Finally, I would want to just give up and not want to do it anymore.

The irony is that this is what the enemy wanted me to do in the first place - ***to give up***. Now, had I given in at that point, the fear of failure almost would have been a self-fulfilling prophesy (*"For the thing which I greatly feared is come upon me, and that which I was afraid of is come unto me."* [Job 3:25]). Getting me to give up would have served a two-fold purpose for the enemy: First, it would have kept me from completing the current assignment. Secondly - and, possibly more importantly - it would have kept me from completely any subsequent assignments and walking out my calling or purpose.

Because faith is the opposite of fear, whenever we sense the fear of failure creeping into our minds and spirits, we must rebuke it and speak the Word of God over our minds, and over our walk. This Word can be anything that the Lord has spoken to you directly, or, in the written scriptures. When we do this, we take on the mind of Christ (Philippians 2:5) and we begin to think like God thinks. At that point, we begin to see ourselves - in both the present and in the future - as God sees us (*"For now we see through a glass, darkly; but then face to face: now I know in part; but then shall I know even as also I am known"* [I Corinthians 13:12]). Then, we will be able to stand on the Word of God for our plans and know that we will be successful.

Below are some scriptures we can read when we are battling the fear of failure:

> *For I know the thoughts that I think toward you, saith the LORD, thoughts of peace, and not of evil, to give you an expected end.* - **Jeremiah 29:11**

> *Jesus said unto him, If thou canst believe, all things are possible to him that believeth.* - **Mark 9:23**

> *And Jesus looking upon them saith, With men it is impossible, but not with God: for with God all things are possible.* – **Mark 10:17**

> *And David said to Solomon his son, Be strong and of good courage, and do it: fear not, nor be dismayed: for the LORD God, even my God, will be with thee; he will not fail thee, nor forsake thee, until thou hast finished all the work for the service of the house of the LORD.*
> **– I Chronicles 28:20**

> *When thou passest through the waters, I will be with thee; and through the rivers, they shall not overflow thee: when thou walkest through the fire, thou shalt not be burned; neither shall the flame kindle upon thee.* – **Isaiah 43:2**

> *What shall we then say to these things? If God be for us, who can be against us?*

> *He that spared not his own Son, but delivered him up for us all, how shall he not with him also freely give us all things?* – **Romans 8:31-32**

SCARE TACTICS: MANIFESTATIONS OF FEAR

In the previous section, we discussed the fear of rejection and the fear of failure. We have also talked about fear and faith and gave examples of both. The last portion of this chapter will be dedicated to discussing the following possible manifestations of fear in the lives of Believers: ***Scared Silly, Scared Speechless, Scared Stiff, Scared to Death*** and ***Scared Straight***.

Scared Silly

The word *silly* can be found three times in scripture (Job 5:2, Hosea 7:11 and II Timothy 3:6). In Job 5:2 and Hosea 7:11, the word *silly* comes from the Hebrew word *pathah,* which has a very lengthy definition. It is shown below:

1 to be spacious, be open, be wide
a (Qal) to be spacious or open or wide
b (Hiphil) to make spacious, make open
2 to be simple, entice, deceive, persuade
a (Qal)
1 to be open-minded, be simple, be naive
2 to be enticed, be deceived
b (Niphal) to be deceived, be gullible
c (Piel)
1 to persuade, seduce
2 to deceive
d (Pual)
1 to be persuaded
2 to be deceived

From the first part of the definition, we see that *pathah,* or, *silly,* means, "*to be spacious or open or wide*" or, "*to make spacious, make open*". This definition coincides with the definition of *pathah* that is in the Gesenius' Hebrew and Chaldee Lexicon to the Old Testament Scriptures[1]. However, in the lexicon, it is clarified even further. Entry one in the lexicon shows that ***the word pathah actually comes from the same root word as the word for talebearer.*** It gives the example of Proverbs 20:19, which reads as follows:

> *He that goeth about as a talebearer revealeth secrets: therefore meddle not with him that flattereth with his lips.*

The lexicon citations says that *pathah,* like ***talebearer,*** indicates *"'one who opens his lips', used of a garrulous man whose lips are continually opening".* ***In other words, a silly person talks too much***!

Fear can cause us to talk too much. When we are afraid, if we are not careful, we may say things we would not normally say and did not intend to say. This could come in the form of talebearing (*revealing secrets, either our own or those with whom others have entrusted us*), gossiping or lying. It could also manifest in speaking word curses on ourselves. Word curses are any *negative thing that is contrary to the Word of God or to the Promises of God for our lives.*

When I was diagnosed with thyroid cancer, my best friend Adrian made sure that when we spoke about the diagnosis in any shape or form - treatments, scans, tests, symptoms, etc. - that we were careful to not speak word curses over the situation and, instead, to only speak God's Promises and the Word over the situation. Adrian is a prophetic intercessor and has both a healing and a teaching ministry. She is a "word curses watchdog". Having been healed of various ailments herself (her testimony is shared extensively in *Chapter T: Thorns*), she knows the value of not giving place to the devil and literally writing your own death certificate - physically, spiritually, psychologically, financially - by what you say. She is also quite knowledgeable about the various healing scriptures. When I would slip and say, "**my** diagnosis" or "**my** type of cancer", or anything else that would denote that I had **accepted ownership** of the illness, Adrian would quickly correct me and would say, "We negate those words and render them powerless, in the Name of Jesus." Sometimes, she would say, "Don't accept that! You are HEALED in the Name of Jesus." She did this because she understood the power of the spoken word, especially out of the mouth of a person who is both a Believer and a true prophet (as with Samuel, my "words do not fall to the ground" [I Samuel 3:19]). Adrian also understood that, because the Word said that God wants us healed (I Peter 2:24), to say anything contrary to that would be ***silly***; to say anything contrary to what God said would be a ***word curse***.

Adrian did not miss a beat, either! She was consistent in correcting me when I would say things that were even borderline word curses. Pretty soon, she had increased my awareness of what I allowed to come out of my mouth, even and especially through that "scary" time. I love and appreciate her so much; her being dogmatic about my developing appropriate/effective speaking habits may have saved my life! Even though *the cancer with which I was diagnosed* (i.e., not "**my**" type of cancer) is the slowest spreading type of thyroid cancer, people have still died from it! And, with the calling that is on my life, the enemy would love to get his hands on me ("*And the Lord said, Simon, Simon, behold, Satan hath desired to have you, that he may sift you as wheat...*" [Luke 22:31]). He won't be able to because I stand on the Word and in faith; Adrian reminded me of this when she admonished me about watching what I say ("*But I have prayed for thee, that thy faith fail not: and when thou art converted, strengthen thy brethren*" [Luke 22:32]). Speaking word curses against myself would merely open a portal for the enemy to enter and would, in fact, **empower** the enemy to come against me. Because God loved me so much that He sent my friend - my sister - to correct me in love ("*For whom the Lord loveth he chasteneth,* *and scourgeth every son whom he receiveth"*. [Hebrews 12:6]). I received the correction and am the better for it.

Word curses are the antithesis of what God has said to us. In John 6:63 c-e, (*"...the words that I speak unto you, they are spirit, and they are life"*), Jesus says that what He said is "life". So, then, in speaking word curses - i.e., *speaking something other that what God has said to us* - we are speaking death to ourselves. Sometimes the death we are speaking can be a physical death; sometimes it can be a spiritual death. Because of this, word curses are detrimental to the successful completion of our walking out our purpose or calling.

But, why do we as Christians speak word curses when we are scared? The answer to this can be found in the second part of the definition of *pathah*.

The composite meanings of *pathah* in the second part of the definition are: *to be simple, to be enticed, to be deceived, to be persuaded, to be open-minded* and *to be gullible*. Remember that ***fear is the absence of faith***. And, fear ***is believing that something or someone will cause us harm***. Without faith, we have a fear of the enemy. In fact, when we are afraid, we are believing the enemy and doubting God. So, then, when we are scared silly, we are easily deceived, enticed and persuaded. We are open-minded to the lies of the enemy and gullible to his tricks and snares. We readily believe what he has told us about ourselves (whether he speaks it to us or uses others to impart his lies about us into our spirits). It is no wonder, then, that when we are scared silly, we believe and speak word curses over our lives. We endanger our spiritual success by doing so.

Not only will we say silly things when we are scared silly, but, God showed that being afraid often causes people to make bad decisions. A person who is afraid may make hasty decisions that are not well thought out and that he or she would not normally make if he or she were not afraid. The result may be that the person would make silly, immature decisions that will affect his or her walk and possibly hinder or thwart the destinies of others.

Consider the following passage of scripture:

> *And there was a famine in the land: and Abram went down into Egypt to sojourn there; for the famine was grievous in the land.*
>
> *And it came to pass, when he was come near to enter into Egypt, that he said unto Sarai his wife, Behold now, I know that thou art a fair woman to look upon:*
>
> *Therefore it shall come to pass, when the Egyptians shall see thee, that they shall say, This is his wife: and they will kill me, but they will save thee alive.*
>
> *Say, I pray thee, thou art my sister: that it may be well with me for thy sake; and my soul shall live because of thee.*
>
> *And it came to pass, that, when Abram was come into Egypt, the Egyptians beheld the woman that she was very fair.*
>
> *The princes also of Pharaoh saw her, and commended her before Pharaoh: and the woman was taken into Pharaoh's house.*
>
> *And he entreated Abram well for her sake: and he had sheep, and oxen, and he asses, and menservants, and maidservants, and she asses, and camels.*

And the LORD plagued Pharaoh and his house with great plagues because of Sarai Abram's wife.

And Pharaoh called Abram, and said, What is this that thou hast done unto me? why didst thou not tell me that she was thy wife?

Why saidst thou, She is my sister? so I might have taken her to me to wife: now therefore behold thy wife, take her, and go thy way.

And Pharaoh commanded his men concerning him: and they sent him away, and his wife, and all that he had.
- Genesis 12: 10-20

In this passage of scripture, there was a famine in the land and Abram and Sarai (later to become Abraham and Sarah) went to Egypt. On his way there, Abram begins to fear for his safety. Abram - who would come to be known as the Father of Faith - was ***scared*** that Pharaoh (i.e., spiritually speaking, the enemy) would harm him in order to take Sarai from him (verses 10-13). He therefore concocts a lie and instructed Sarai to lie, too. Abram told Sarai to say that she was his sister and, by implication, that she was not his wife. The lie was not that Sarai was his sister, because in fact there was some truth to that statement (she was his half-sister; they shared the same father but had different mothers [Gen. 20:12]). To imply that she was not his wife was, in fact, acting deceptively. Abram allowed fear to cause him to make a ***silly*** decision and to act in a ***silly*** manner. He also influenced Sarai to act in a ***silly*** manner; all to save himself, rather than trust God - the same God who instructed him to "*Get thee out of thy country, and from thy kindred, and from thy father's house, unto a land that I will shew thee* "(Genesis 12:1) - to take care of him. God even confirmed that He would bless Abram and "make his name great" (Genesis 12:2-3). Abram was on an assignment from God and still did not have faith that God would protect him!

The fact that Abraham lied and instructed Sarai to lie was bad enough. However, in verse 17, we see that Pharaoh - acting on the misinformation he received from Abram and Sarai - was plagued by the Lord because he housed Sarai, Abram's lawful wife. So, then, Abram's fear - ***being scared silly and therefore telling a lie*** - had affected Sarai and "Pharaoh and his house."

And, if it would have only stopped there, then the story itself might not be so significant. But, consider this: What would have happened if, instead of Pharaoh realizing that God was plaguing him and his house because of Sarai's presence in verse 18, that Pharaoh said nothing and kept Sarai as one of his wives? Then, Sarai may never have become Sarah, and she and Abram may not have begotten Isaac, because they would no longer have been together. Had that happened, there would have been no Jacob. Without Jacob, it is possible Judah and the heads of the Tribes of Israel might not have existed (Matthew 1:2). Without Judah and his descendants, there might not have been a Boaz (Matt. 1:3-5). If there were no Boaz, there may not be a Jesse (Matthew 1:5). Without Jesse, David may not have been born (Matthew 1:6). And, if there were no David and his lineage, the Messiah may not have come (Mathew 1:6-16), or at least not through that lineage!

We have no idea how many people will be ministered to as a result of our walk. I personally am finding out that people that I don't even know have read ***When*** (from the initial printing) and were greatly ministered to by it. This is great, considering only 250 copies of it were put into circulation in the initial printing, and I *knew* the people into whom I sowed the copies. How the books got into the hands of people all over the country is beyond my knowledge, except that the Bible declares. "*So shall my word be that goeth forth out of my mouth: it shall not return unto me void, but it shall accomplish that which I please, and it shall prosper [in the thing] whereto I sent it.*" (Isaiah 55:11). We just never really know who we are reaching and teaching, even if just by our example. The obverse side of that, though, is that we have no idea how many people may never be reached or may be negatively impacted if we do not walk in our calling. Our being scared silly may hinder our walk, or it may hinder the walks of people - those we may never know - for generations to come.

Scared Speechless

There is another manifestation of fear in which the person experiencing it is not able to speak. In the physical realm, the phenomenon is called **psychosomatic laryngitis**. Psychosomatic means, "*(of a physical illness or other condition) caused or aggravated by a mental factor such as internal conflict or stress, of or relating to the interaction of mind and body.*" Laryngitis is, "*inflammation of the larynx, typically resulting in huskiness or loss of the voice, harsh breathing, and a painful cough.*" The larynx is the voice box; it is the apparatus in the body through which vocal sound is produced with aid of the vocal cords. Psychosomatic laryngitis, then, means *a huskiness or loss of the voice that was either caused or aggravated by conflict or stress.* In short, a person with psychosomatic laryngitis experiences a trauma or stress of some sort, and the mind tells the body that the larynx cannot function properly for the person to speak.

The concept of spiritual psychosomatic laryngitis will be discussed in greater detail in, ***Through My Roaring,*** book four of the ***Roaring*** series. But, for our current discussion, *spiritual psychosomatic laryngitis* is ***a manifestation of fear, which can cause us to be scared speechless***. This is different than being scared silly because when we are scared silly we talk too much and say the wrong thing. However, when we are scared speechless, we do not use our "voice." Operating in fear, we simply sit back and "say" nothing.

God instructed me to stress that spiritual psychosomatic laryngitis is **not** the same as being struck speechless by the Lord. In fact, it is the direct opposite. There are instances in the Bible where, for various and sundry reasons, God chose to strike people "dumb" - unable to speak. In Luke 1:20, Zacharias, the father of John the Baptist, was struck dumb by God because he did not believe God's Promises to him regarding fathering a child - John the Baptist - at his age. He was unable to speak until after the baby was born. Zacharias' inability to speak was **orchestrated by God**. Spiritual psychosomatic laryngitis, however, is a manifestation of fear and is therefore orchestrated by the enemy.

Spiritual psychosomatic laryngitis is a ploy of the enemy to silence the voices of Believers. The word voice, as it appears in the Bible, comes from the Hebrew word *qowl* and the Greek word *phone*. The definitions of both words are very similar. Both *qowl* and *phone* mean, *"voice, sound, tone - produced by humans, animals and inanimate objects"*.

Each human's voice has characteristic that makes his or her voice unique. This is because the vocal apparatuses (larynx, vocal cords, tongue, teeth, nasal cavities through which sound travels) are unique to each person. That is why we can use voice-activated devices such as cell phones and GPS navigational systems; when we set the system up, we programmed the device using its voice recognition system. The device will activate when it recognizes our unique voice and perform the appropriate function. Therefore, while each Believer has a voice, each Believer's voice is distinctly different. Our spiritual apparatuses - *the anointings and callings/walks* - are distinct and different.

God also has a distinctive, unique voice. We as Believers must learn to hear and recognize His Voice:

> *Give unto the LORD the glory due unto his name; worship the LORD in the beauty of holiness.*
>
> *The **voice** of the LORD is upon the waters: the God of glory thundereth: the LORD is upon many waters.*
>
> *The **voice** of the LORD is powerful; the voice of the LORD is full of majesty.*
>
> *The **voice** of the LORD breaketh the cedars; yea, the LORD breaketh the cedars of Lebanon.*
>
> *He maketh them also to skip like a calf; Lebanon and Sirion like a young unicorn.*
>
> *The **voice** of the LORD divideth the flames of fire.*
>
> *The **voice** of the LORD shaketh the wilderness; the LORD shaketh the wilderness of Kadesh.*
>
> *The **voice** of the LORD maketh the hinds to calve, and discovereth the forests: and in his temple doth every one speak of his glory.* - **Psalms 29: 2-9**
>
> *My sheep hear my voice, and I know them, and they follow me.* – **John 10:27**

What is the sound, then, or tone that Believers make/produce? In what way(s) do we use our voices for God's glory, for our spiritual growth advancement and for the edification of the Kingdom of God? And, why is being scared speechless a danger?

In the Scared Silly section, we discussed John 6:63 c-e, which says, *"...the words that I speak unto you, they are spirit, and they are life"*. These words were spoken by Jesus. And, we know that miracles were wrought by Jesus' **spoken words**. In Mark 5:10-20, He **commanded** the legion of demons to come out of the demon-possessed man and commanded them to go into the swine. In John 11:43, he **spoke** to then-deceased Lazarus and **commanded** him to come forth from the grave. In Mark 5:41, he **spoke** to the centurion's daughter and raised her from the dead. So, then, clearly, Jesus' **words were the vehicles through which He wrought mighty works**. Jesus also said, *"Verily, verily, I say unto **you**, He that believeth on me, the works that I do shall he do also; and greater [works] than these shall he do; because I go unto my Father."*(John 14:12) The "you" is the True Church; the Believers. If Jesus' **words** were used to do great works, and we are supposed to do those works and greater, then, ***our words are powerful and essential to the manifestation of Kingdom power and authority.***

Many of those mighty works can be manifested through praise, which also requires a voice. In fact, praise has many "voices". Because a voice can be a spoken voice (as in a human, with a larynx) or a sound or tone from an inanimate object, praise can take the form of a spoken praise (Genesis 29:35), a sung praise (I Chronicles 16:23) or a musical instrument (Psalms 149:3), to name a few. Our blessings, breakthroughs, healings, deliverances and victories require voice activation and, many times, will only "recognize" the voice of praise to line up with God's

Will for our lives. The role of praise in the lives of Believers can in no way be minimized. In fact, God was so emphatic about praise being brought forth from the earth realm until, in Luke 19:40, He said that if we, the Believers, do not praise Him that the stones/rocks would cry out in our place! It is no surprise, then, that the enemy would use fear to paralyze our spiritual larynx so that we cannot produce praise! He knows that, as the old adage says, "When the praises go up, the blessings come down." He also knows that our praises - spoken, vocal or musical - serve as the soundtrack for our spiritual walk.

Mighty works can also be wrought through using our voices for ministry. Ministry, for purposes of this discussion, is defined as, "*the work or vocation of a minister of religion; the spiritual work or service of any Christian or a group of Christians, esp. evangelism.*" Some of these ministerial functions can include preaching (II Timothy 2:4), teaching (Deuteronomy 11:5), evangelizing (II Timothy 4:5), witnessing (Acts 1:8), testifying (Luke 16:28), rebuking (Mark 8:32), encouraging (Isaiah 41:7), speaking in tongues, known and unknown (Acts 2:4), interpreting tongues (I Corinthians 12:10), praying (I Thessalonians 5:17) interceding (Romans 11:2) and prophesying (I Corinthians 14:39). All of these functions (and many more) are necessary parts of the Body of Christ (I Corinthians 12:21-25). When all the parts of the Body are functioning properly, souls will be saved, captives will be set free, demons will be casted out, God's People will walk in power and authority in the earth realm and the Kingdom at large will be empowered and enabled to do God's Will on earth.

It should come as no surprise then, that the enemy tries relentlessly to silence our voices and to have us scared speechless. He knows that whenever we use our voices -

be it for praise or other types of ministry - we become stronger and the Word of God is spread. He does not want this and does everything he can to make sure that we are not able to use our voices to do the bidding of our King.

When I was being diagnosed with thyroid cancer, my endocrinologist did an ultrasound on my thyroid bed. He found a cyst that was about the size of a kalamata olive. The cyst had been there for at least three years of which I was aware. Prior to the diagnosis, I used to suffer from severe allergy problems and sinus infections. I had gone to several doctors for the sinus problems/infections. Both they and I had noticed this cyst. These doctors told me that this was a swollen gland and when the infection cleared up, the "gland" would go down. In May 2009, during a routine physical, my gynecologist noticed the "gland" and became concerned. He told me that it was not a swollen gland, but was, more than likely a cyst. He then referred me to an endocrinologist who would examine my thyroid.

During the thyroid exam, the endocrinologist told me that it was a cyst - not a swollen gland - and that it could be cancerous. I received a fine needle aspiration (where a fine needle was inserted into the cyst, tissues extracted and examined), but the results were "Suspicious", meaning the biopsy could not prove with any certainty that the cyst was or was not cancerous.

The endocrinologist at this point suggested that the cyst be removed. He did this for two reasons. For one thing, the cyst was lying directly against my trachea (wind pipe), my larynx and my vocal cords. I had noticed some hoarseness when I spoke or sang, but, again, I thought this was due to sinus problems/infections. But, because of this, I limited the time I spoke and the amount of singing I did. Before long, I wasn't singing very much at all and I would preach, but the discomfort would interfere with the flow of my ministering. The doctor said that the cyst would, more than likely, keep growing and therefore put more and more pressure on my vocal apparatuses and cut my breathing off. If left unattended, the cyst could grow to a point that it would severely affect my voice and would in all likelihood get to the point where it could cut my breath off in my sleep.

The second reason the endocrinologist recommended having the cyst removed was for esthetics of it; he said that it was noticeable (as it sat on the front left and center portion of my thyroid and looked like a high Adam's apple). He said that as it grew, it would become more unsightly and would possible grow into a goiter.

The third reason he suggested the surgery was because surgery was the only real way to know if the cyst was cancerous. Should I choose to have the surgery, the surgeon would perform thorough biopsy of the thyroid when it was removed to determine if there were cancer cells present. If so, then I could take measures to eradicate any cancer cells in my body; and this would be done with radioactive iodine pill treatments.

I prayed about it, talked with my husband and Adrian about it. I decided to have the surgery. Prior to the surgery, I met with the surgeon to discuss the surgery and so that he could let me know what to expect. The surgeon told me that while a thyroidectomy – *the removal of the thyroid* – is a fairly simple operation. But, he said, there are some potential dangers of which he, by law, had to make me aware. Particularly, he had to let me know that because the thyroid touches the larynx and vocal cords, there have been instances in which people who have had a thyroidectomy have had their vocal cords nicked or severed! When this happens, the person's voice is either gone forever or the person's vocal ability diminishes greatly. He said that permanent vocal cord damage is not common, but it does happen; it is a risk and, by law, he had to inform me of the risk. He also said that nearly everyone who has a thyroidectomy will have hoarseness and will have somewhat diminished vocal cord capacity for a few weeks or months. I had read about this and had heard that it **could** last for as long as a year, but that the vocal cords would eventually strengthen and the voice would go back to normal.

Armed with this new knowledge, I again had to make a decision regarding having the thyroidectomy. All my life I have sang - from a child in our Free Will Baptist Church choir until now - and I enjoy it immensely. I also preach, teach and prophesy. To imagine life without talking, singing, preaching, teaching or prophesying was disheartening. Outside of my writing, the talking, singing, preaching, teaching and prophesying were how I used my "voice". I knew that God had ordained me to do these things; I knew I needed to do them to walk out my prophetic purpose and destiny. And, yet, with one felt swoop of the scalpel, my whole life as I knew it could be changed. No more talking, no more singing; no more preaching; no more teaching; no more prophesying.

But, I also knew that I had prayed about this already and God had given me a peace about it. I knew that He would not leave me nor forsake me (Hebrews 13:5), and He watches over His Word to perform it (Jeremiah 1:12). I knew in my spirit that this is God's Ministry with which He has entrusted me - He is in control! God called me from my mother's womb (Jeremiah 1:5). In fact, He made me and formed me and established my purpose even before the foundations of the earth! And, *"he which hath begun a good work in you will perform [it] until the day of Jesus*

Christ"(Phil. 1:16)! With that confidence I re-decided and went ahead with plans for the surgery.

The surgery went well. The surgeon removed the thyroid and sent it off to be biopsied. When I awoke from the four-hour procedure, I was in the recovery room. The nurse asked me if I were okay. She **spoke** to me, and her questions required an answer. I **could have** shaken my head yes or no, but, I **wanted** to use my voice. Without hesitation, I **said**, "Yes!" My voice, although a little hoarse, was as clear as a bell! That night - a few hours after the surgery - I sang, praised God, talk to the nurses, carried on conversations with family members and phone conversations with friends; I had my VOICE! I spent the night in the hospital and was released the next day. When the surgeon came to check on me, he was astonished as to how strong my voice was! He said it was unheard of for someone to be able to talk and sing right after surgery like I did. I told him that all praises and honor went to God. In telling him about the goodness of the Lord, I **ministered**! I used **my voice**.

And, it didn't stop there! I felt an unction in my spirit to prophesy to one of the nurses who came in to check on me. The Lord moved right there in the hospital room and ministered a powerful prophetic word to her concerning some family issues that had been grieving her. She said she had been praying and had asked the Lord to speak to her concerning some decisions she had to make. She believed that the Lord had sent me to minister to her with just the right word and just the right time!

A few days later, my voice began to get raspy and hoarse. I still had a strong talking voice most of the time, but my singing voice got shaky. The enemy tried to get my attention and tell me that my voice would never be the same. But, I knew that he is a liar! I have had to learn to use wisdom and to not overtax my vocal cords; when I am tired, I have to know when to be quiet for a while so that the vocal cords can rest. Because the cyst was so large and had been there so long, it both supported and weakened my vocal cords. When it was gone, my vocal cords on the left side have to be retrained; they had been **traumatized**, both by the cyst being there and by the cyst being removed.

Before I knew it, I had become self-conscious about my singing. I didn't even want to sing anymore because it didn't sound the same to me. With the left vocal cords being weakened, my tone was a little flat or off-key. I would hear myself singing and then all of a sudden stop because it bothered me so that my professionally trained and once nearly pitch-perfect voice had come to this! I was tempted to give into the spirit of fear and abandon singing altogether, but I didn't. I kept singing. ***I didn't allow myself to be scared speechless.***

God is good, though. I never stopped ministering! Even though I have been primarily homebound for nearly a year, I ministered; I used my "voice". God has blessed me to have a tremendous group of people on Facebook to whom I minister. We talk both online and via telephone. I have contacts all over the U.S. and in Australia, the United Kingdom, and in many parts of Africa. I have been invited to come minister all over the world. And, as I am writing this chapter - a month shy of the one-year anniversary of my thyroidectomy - I am **cancer free** and I am preparing to go preach my first speaking engagement since the surgery! I am excited because God prevailed! And, my singing voice is different, but, in some ways, better than before!

God said to tell you to not allow spiritual psychosomatic laryngitis or trauma of any kind to keep you from using your voice. The enemy will bring situations that will seemingly traumatize you and keep you from saying that that God has placed in your spirit to speak, sing or "noise abroad". God said the spirit of fear is a cancerous spirit that will try to attach itself to you; it is sent by the enemy to silence you. When this happens, search your soul, identify the problem, denounce the fear and allow Him to "do surgery" and remove the "cyst". While you are being healed, be sure to continue to "use your voice"; stay in the habit of praising and ministering as the Lord leads, being careful not to overdo by listening to the unction of the Holy Spirit. During your recuperation time, God will give you fresh manna - Divine revelation - and will, at His appointed time, release you to use your voice to share that revelation.

Scared Stiff

A third manifestation of fear in the life of the Believer is a phenomenon called being scared stiff. Being scared stiff is actually a euphemism for a person *being so afraid until he or she loses the ability to move at will.* Non-spiritually speaking, the person who is scared stiff literally freezes up while in a dangerous or scary situation, particularly when the danger is ensuing but has not yet caused the person any immediate harm. Oftentimes, the person who is scared stiff wastes valuable time that he or she could have avoided harm by simply becoming stationary and not doing anything.

An example of being scared stiff would be the following: Perhaps someone is driving a car and sees a semi-truck in the distance that is headed toward him or her at a relatively high speed. A person who is scared stiff may be so petrified that he or she will not even try to get out of the path of the semi-truck but will sit there - frozen and seemingly unable to think or move - and will potentially get hit by the truck.

Being scared stiff is much like being scared speechless, except that being scared stiff affects the mobility of the entire body, while being scared speechless affects only the vocal apparatuses. Spiritually speaking, while being scared speechless affects our "voice" (praise and vocal ministry), being scared stiff affects ***movement***. Although I will elaborate on our "bones" in, ***My Bones Waxed Old***, book three in the ***Roaring*** series, I will say here that being scared stiff causes long period of being stagnant - *immobility* - and this is not good for our spiritual muscles or bones. Being stiff for too long causes a plethora of problems and can eventually result in spiritual death.

When we are scared stiff, we do not move when God tells us to do so. Or, if we do move, we move slowly and not gracefully; we do not flow. As a result, we may miss God's Timing and therefore miss what He wanted to do with us, through us and in us in a particular season. This is important because the Bible declares that, "*To every [thing there is] a season, and a time to every purpose under the heaven*" (Ecclesiastes 3:1). We need to be perfectly synchronized with God's Will and Instructions for our lives. The Bible also declares that, "*For in him we live, and move, and have our being…*" (Acts 17:28a)." Because fear is the antithesis of faith, we cannot be in fear and "live and move and have our being". If we are scared stiff, we are not in faith and cannot move and live and our being in Him.

God reminded me of more experiences during my bout with thyroid cancer and showed me how they further illustrated the concept of being "stiff". One of the side effects I experienced when my hormones fluctuated was joint stiffness. My hands, fingers, knees and legs were stiff and were in pain. As a result, when God spoke to me and told me to resume writing, it took me a while to get a flow going at first. It was not that I was not willing to be obedient. It was not that I did not have a "voice"; I knew what He wanted me to say and I wanted to say it. But, my flow was hindered because of the stiffness and the pain! My fingers would hurt as I typed; the stiffness of the fingers made it difficult to type accurately and as swiftly as I used to type. My hands would hurt from using the mouse on the computer. My wrists would hurt from being bent for periods of time. My knees and legs would hurt from sitting so long at the computer and would be even stiffer when I got up and walked around.

I made a conscious decision, though, that I was going to press through and to finish the writing assignments that the Lord had given me, especially after a nine-year delay. Once I decided to press through, the Lord blessed me and my doctor found that I was taking the wrong dosage of hormones. Once I got my hormones closer to being balanced and once I just started typing, even through the pain and stiffness, the stiffness and pain subsided.

God said that being scared stiff prevents us from "doing." God wants us to have faith, but we must also **do**. The Bible declares that, "*Faith without works is dead*" (James 2:26). When we are scared stiff, it is not that we don't have any faith, but we do not have enough faith and/or our faith is misdirected. Therefore, we do not do, what we are supposed to do. As with the natural body, if we do not move, we eventually bring death to the body. Being scared stiff is the precursor to spiritual death.

Scared to Death

Being scared to death is the fourth manifestation of fear in the life of the Believer that we will discuss. Quite simply put, being scared to death means *to be so affected by fear until one dies from it*. In the physical sense, this could be someone having a fatal heart attack after being frightened. In the spiritual sense, being scared to death means allowing fear to take such precedence in one's mind until he or she dies a spiritual death rather than face the fear and/or the object of the fear.

Being scared stiff is the precursor for being scared to death. Physically speaking, prolonged periods of immobility cause all parts of the body to suffer and will eventually result in death. Also, when a person suffers a fatal massive coronary, the heart either freezes up or does not beat correctly, resulting in death. Spiritually speaking, the Bible tells us that Satan comes as a roaring lion, seeking whom he may devour (I Peter 5:8). It also tells us that the devil comes to kill, to steal and to destroy (John 10:10). Satan's ultimate plan for us is to kill us; he especially desires for us to die a spiritual death. It is not unrealistic, then, that he would use the fear(s) that we harbor or entertain to be the vehicle through which spiritual death comes. If we are spiritually dead, we cannot walk out our prophetic purpose or calling.

To avoid being scared to death, we must always be mindful of our heart. The Bible tells us to "*Keep thy heart with all diligence; for out of it [are] the issues of life*" (Proverbs 4:23). Our heart is our mind. The Bible also says to, "*let his mind be in you which was also in Christ Jesus, who thought it not robbery to be equal with God*" (Philippians 2:5-6). In order for Jesus to think that it was not robbery (i.e., not blasphemous; that it was okay) to be equal with God, Jesus had to have a concept of Himself as God. Jesus knew who He was! We, too, have to know who we are in Christ; we have to know that we are " a chosen generation, a royal priesthood" (I Peter 2:9). We have to know that we are heirs of God and joint heirs with Christ (Romans 8:17). We have to know that no weapon formed against us shall prosper and every tongue that rises up against us in judgment we shall condemn (Isaiah 54:17). We have to know this, but we have to know it ***by faith***. When this is rhema to us, no situation the enemy can throw at us can cause us to fear anyone or anything to death!

SCARED STRAIGHT:
THE RIGHT KIND OF FEAR; THE DESIRED MANIFESTATION

So far, we have discussed fear as being *"an unpleasant emotion caused by the belief that someone or something is dangerous, likely to cause pain or a threat."* Fear, based on this most common definition of fear, is the antithesis of faith in God. We have also discussed different types of fear based on this definition as well as manifestations of this definition of fear in the lives of Believers. However, returning to our complete definition of fear, we see that there is a fourth definition of fear. This definition says that fear means, *"regard God with reverence and awe"*. In other words, this is ***the fear of the Lord***.

The Hebrew word for this same type of fear - ***the fear of the Lord*** - is *yira*, and its definition is as follows:

1 fear, terror, fearing
- *a fear, terror*
- *b awesome or terrifying thing (object causing fear)*
- *c fear (of God), respect, reverence, piety*
- *d revered*

The Greek word for the fear of the Lord is *fobos* (*phobos*) is as follows:

1 fear, dread, terror (that which strikes terror)

2 reverence for one's husband

When we as Believers fear the Lord, we are saying that we have ***faith*** in and ***respect for*** His Omnipotence and Omnipresence (II Chronicles 16:9). We know that He is Alpha and Omega (Revelations 1:8); we ***believe*** that He is Jehovah Jireh, the God who provides (Genesis 22:14); we know that He is Jehovah Shalom, the Prince of Peace (Judges 6:22-24). We ***believe*** all that the Word has said about Him and all that we have come to know of Him through our experiences with Him. And, because we ***believe*** this, we are ***in awe of him*** (as the fourth part of the definition of fear says) and we have a ***belief*** that being without Him would expose us to the wiles of the devil (Ephesians 6:11), which would "***likely cause pain or a threat***" (part one of the definition of fear). We ***revere*** Him. We ***respect*** Him. And, in this sense of the definition, ***we fear Him***.

And, because we love and revere Him, we keep His Commandments ("*If ye love me, keep my commandments*" [John 14:15]). As we keep His Commandments, we stay on the path of righteousness ("*...he leadeth me in the paths of righteousness for his name's sake.*" [Psalms 23:3b]), and we walk the way of the Lord, a straight and narrow way ("*Because strait [is] the gate, and narrow [is] the way, which leadeth unto life, and few there be that find it*" [Matthew 7:14]). At that point, our only desire is to please God. ***At that point, we are scared straight***.

Getting scared straight for the Lord is a manifestation of the fear of the Lord in the life of the Believer and is a necessity to a successful walk with the Lord. Once we reach the scared straight stage in our walk, God can reveal more of His Mysteries to us. At that point, we are sold out to Him, yielded to His every instruction to us. It is no wonder, then, that Psalms 11:10 says the following:

> *The fear of the LORD [is] the beginning of wisdom: a good understanding have all they that do [his commandments]: his praise endureth for ever.*

Putting It All Together

When writing this chapter, I considered writing various chapters about other possible hinderances to ones walk. However, after I began writing this chapter, I realized that most of the ones I considered writing about really had roots in fear. Fear plays a major role in several other emotions we experience and is a gateway spirit for other spirits to enter and wreak havoc in our spiritual lives. Having explored fear, we found that it is the antithesis of faith. We also discussed ways in which fear manifests in the life of the Believer. To decrease or eradicate any fear, we must feed our faith and increase it. We can do this by hearing the Word of God (Romans 10:17). Because God is love (I John 4:8) and perfect love casts out fear (I John 4:18), when we secure and solidify our relationship with Him on a daily basis - through spending time with Him in the word, prayer and communing with him - we keep the spirit of fear at bay and greatly decrease our chances of being scared, or being afraid of the enemy. We can then live life in the fullness of God, complete with His Peace and Love.

[1]"Pathah/Silly". *Genesius' Hebrew and Chaldee Lexicon to the Old Testament Scriptures.* 1884. Print.

I

Imagination

Creativity is an extension of our spiritual giftings and callings. Creativity is also a characteristic of God, and a prophetic, spiritual trait that is passed on from the Father to us, the children. The Bible says that God spoke the world as we know it into existence. So, then, all that is was created by the Word of God (Genesis 1). And, in the previous chapter of this book—Chapter S: Scared—we learned of our ability to speak things—positive and negative—into existence. But, we can also create in other ways. God has blessed us with many talents (writing, singing, drawing, acting, building, to name a few), all of which are outlets for our creativity. These areas can be a tremendous blessing to the Kingdom of God if channeled correctly and used to the Glory of God.

And, when one studies creativity, the word *imagination* often comes to mind. Some people believe that imagination plays a direct role in a person's creativity. In fact, some people say that imagination is the only factor in the creative process. I heard this said and something quickened in my spirit. I prayed about this and God began to deal with me concerning imagination and the role that it should play in the life of the Christian. God gave me a revelation concerning imagination and told me to write about it as the subject of this chapter.

I researched imagination as it pertained to Christians. I must admit; I found many sources written by people who would disagree with what God showed me. Nevertheless, I know what He said to me about it. I discussed these points with a group of ministers and was told that, what He gave me may not be for everyone, particularly not for non-prophetic people (that was an eye-opener for me; I will discuss that later). But, because He led me to write this chapter, I believe that the revelation He gave me will minister to others. That revelation is as follows: ***While I am not convinced that imagination is key to creativity, I am certain that it may in some ways hinder the walk of the Believer and serve to silence our giftings and callings***.

That being said, I will approach this chapter a little differently than I have any other I have written thus far. After defining imagination and discussing tools our mind uses to help us make associations, I will begin by discussing what the Lord showed me about imagination. Those will be my discussion points. Then, I will list and discuss counterpoints made by people whose beliefs about imagination are somewhat different than mine, so that I will discuss points that do not necessarily support what God showed me. I am doing this under the direction of the Holy Spirit because God wants to correct and/or shed light on our thinking process(-es) and on the process(-es) of how He speaks to us. After that, I will list and discuss my counter to the counterpoint, as God revealed it to me. At the end of this chapter, I will discuss a point upon which myself, the other ministers and all the writers of the sources I researched are all agreed: ***Ungodly imagination is destructive and detrimental to a successful spiritual walk; it silences the Believer.***

WHAT IS IMAGINATION?

Let's begin by defining imagination. In the dictionary, the word ***imagination*** means, *"the faculty or action of forming new ideas, or images or concepts of external objects not present to the senses."* Within the scope of this definition are two other variations on this same theme. They are as follows: *"the ability of the mind to be creative or resourceful"* and *"the part of the mind that imagines things."* In the Bible, the Hebrew words for imagination are, ***yetse*** and ***sheriyruwth***. ***Yetse*** has to do with *forming an intellectual framework*. ***Sheriyruwth*** refers to *a stubbornness, a hardening – a hardness of heart*. The Greek word for imagination is *dianoia*, and means, *"the mind as a faculty of understanding, feeling or desire; a way of thinking and feeling; thoughts, either good or bad."*

Our English word imagination comes from the root word ***imagine***. The definition of ***imagine*** is, *"form a mental picture or a concept of."* It also means, *"believe (something unreal) to be so"* and, *"suppose or assume."* The Hebrew words for ***imagine*** are ***chasab***, (*to think, plan, esteem, calculate, invent, make a judgment, imagine, count*), ***chamac*** (*to wrong, do violence to, treat violently, do wrongly*), ***hagah*** (*to moan, growl, utter, muse, mutter, meditate, devise, plot, speak*), ***hathath*** (*to moan, growl, utter, muse, mutter, meditate, devise, plot, speak*), ***charash*** (*to cut in, plough, engrave, devise; to be silent, be dumb, be speechless, be deaf*). ***Meletao*** is the Greek word for ***imagine*** and it means, *"to care for, attend to carefully, practise; to meditate i.e. to devise, contrive."*

Imagine is, of course, derived from the word ***image***. There are many definitions for the word ***image***, but the one that is appropriate for this chapter is, *"a mental representation or idea."* Likewise, there are several Hebrew and Greek definitions of the word ***image***. The most common one is the Hebrew word *tselem*. This is the one used in Genesis 1:26a-b *("And God said, Let us make man in our image, after our likeness....")*. It means,*"image: **a)** images (of tumours, mice, heathen gods)**b)** image, likeness (of resemblance) **c)** mere, empty, image, semblance (fig.)"*.

Imagination and Its Workings in the Mind

Returning to the definition of imagination, it is "*the faculty or action of forming new ideas, or images or concepts of external objects not present to the senses*". It also means "*the ability of the mind to be creative or resourceful*" and "*the part of the mind that imagines things.*" So, then, the **mind is forming new ideas, images or concepts**. But, how does the mind do this? To answer this question, let's turn to the field of elementary education and borrow/apply some of its terms.

In elementary education (grades Kindergarten through sixth), teachers build foundational skills (basic reading [comprehension and application], writing [spelling, grammar, handwriting], and arithmetic [addition, subtraction, division, multiplication, fractions, decimals, time telling and money counting]). The process begins in Kindergarten with the teacher teaching the basics: number recognition, counting, alphabet recognition and sounds, colors, etc. When the student masters these skills, he or she has successfully mastered the content for that particular grade level and is promoted to the next grade - first grade. In first grade, the teacher may introduce new curriculum, but it is always based on some skill that the child learned in Kindergarten. Once the child successfully masters the first grade curriculum, he or she is promoted to second grade, where newer, more challenging curriculum is taught, but it always has its basis in what was taught in the previous two grades. And so the story goes. With each level, the student is taught different strategies to help them learn new materials. These strategies are called tools. Let's now explore these tools in even greater detail.

Tool: Prior Knowledge

Sophie is a first grader. She is also a cat lover and has a pet cat, Fluffy. The previous year, Sophie's Kindergarten teacher taught the class that, "C is for cat. C says, 'kuh-kuh-kuh' but a cat says, 'Meow!" Now Sophie is in the beginning of her first grade year and has to read on her own. Sophie is learning simple sight words. She has never seen the word **meow** before. Sophie's teacher shows her the following passage and asks her to read it aloud.

Jill has a cat. Jill's cat says, "Meow."

Let's suppose that Sophie reads all the words correctly except "meow" (i.e., having never seen the word "meow" before stumbles on that word.) Let's suppose that she tries again, but cannot read it/sound it out.

The teacher then asks Sophie:
"What sound does Jill's cat make?"

How would Sophie go about ascertaining the answer to this question? First of all, Sophie is a cat lover and has her pet cat Fluffy at home. She is used to being around Fluffy and has probably heard Fluffy makes cat noises. Secondly, Sophie's Kindergarten teacher taught her that, "C is for cat. C says, 'kuh, kuh, kuh", but a cat says, 'Meow!'" So, then, even if Sophie had never seen the word meow before, she could glean from what she learned in the past at school (Kindergarten) or from what she has experienced in the past with Fluffy (at home). The pool of acquired knowledge from which Sophie can draw and then apply to answer the question is called ***prior knowledge***.

Tool: Context Clues

A different scenario is as follows: Jasmine is a second grader. She is reading the following story and will have to answer questions when she finishes:

> *Animals are our pets, but animals can also help us in many ways. They can even help the police.* ***Canines****, such as Dalmatians and other dogs, help firemen, policemen and even assist the elderly and the blind.*

Question:
What does canines mean?

To answer this question, Jasmine would have to realize that the word ***canines***, is followed by the phrase, "***such as Dalmatians and other dogs.***" She would have to pull on prior knowledge to remember that ***as*** is like "equals" (something normally taught in the first grade). Then, she would deduce that if canines are equal to Dalmatians and the sentence says, "***...Dalmatians and other dogs...***", then a Dalmatian must be a dog, because the word ***other*** means that whatever preceded it is like unto or in the same "group" as the word that follows it (this is usually learned in first grade, too). And, if a Dalmatian is a dog and is equal to canines, then, ***canines must mean dogs***. Jasmine would be able to answer the question correctly by getting clues as to what the word meant by looking at the surrounding words – by examining the context in which the canines was used. This is called using ***context clues***.

Tool: Inference

The last scenario I will give from the field of elementary education is as follows: Roberto, a third grader, is reading the following passage and must answer the question beneath it:

Thomas was so sad that he had forgotten his umbrella today. In a rush to get to school on time, he ran out of the house with his shoes untied, his hair frazzled and his face covered with grape jelly from breakfast. He ran outside and got drenched! He arrived at school, soaking wet. Grey, cloudy skies always made him melancholy, and being soaked and cold didn't help much, either. "I should have listened to the weather forecast for today, "Thomas thought to himself as he sloshed into Mrs. Sapphire's first period class…late as usual.

Question:
More than likely, how did Thomas get wet?

To answer this question, Roberto would certainly have to use ***prior knowledge*** of when to use an umbrella. He might be able to draw from the ***context clues***, seeing words such as ***drenched, soaking and sloshed*** - *all of which mean wet* - but one can get drenched, soaked and sloshed in many different ways (fire hose, flooded apartment, water balloon fight, to name a few). Thomas would have to remember from the passage that Thomas ran outside without an umbrella and that it was outside that he got drenched. Based on Roberto's prior knowledge of when to use an umbrella coupled with the other information in the story, Roberto can form the most logical conclusion based on what is being said to infer what is not being said. Roberto can use a process called ***inference*** to conclude that Thomas got wet in the rain.

DISCUSSION POINT 1:
Imagination Relies on the Mind; the Mind is "Flawed."

God showed me that while imagination may be

beneficial in some respect, it also can be stifling and deceptive. Imagination ("*the faculty or action of forming new ideas, or images or concepts of external objects not present to the senses*") relies on the mind because ideas are formed in the mind. And, the mind relies on prior knowledge, context clues and inference (among other tools) to make connections and form new ideas, images or concepts. The problem with this as it relates to spiritual matters is that many times **God wants us to do things for which we have no "earthly" prior knowledge, context clues or inference**. Our minds often cannot conceive or perceive spiritual matters ("*But as it is written, Eye hath not seen, nor ear heard, neither have entered into the heart of man, the things which God hath prepared for them that love him.*" [I Corinthians 2:9]). In fact, our minds are, at first (prior to salvation and restoration) carnal, and carnality is enmity against God or an enemy of God ("*Because the carnal mind [is] enmity against God: for it is not subject to the law of God, neither indeed can be.*" [Romans 8:7]).

In scripture, the terms mind and heart are interchangeable; i.e., when the Bible speaks of the heart, it is not speaking of the organ that pumps blood through the body. Otherwise, the physical body could not function with a stony heart (Ezekiel 36:26). Instead, the word *heart* in the Bible means the mind - specifically, the part of the mind where the innermost thoughts, motives and intents are contained. The Bible says, "*The heart [is] deceitful above all [things], and desperately wicked: who can know it?*" (Jeremiah 17:9) So, then, if imaginations come through the mind and the mind is also the heart, and the heart is "desperately wicked", it stands to reason that imaginations may be evil.

The Bible seems to bear out this very thing. In the Bible, the words imagination and imagine and variations of the words (imaginations, imagined and imagineth) appear a combined total of 36 times. Of all those times, there are really only two times when the word imagination is used in a "***non-negative***" connotation (*"O LORD God of Abraham, Isaac, and of Israel, our fathers, keep this for ever in the* **imagination** *of the thoughts of the heart of thy people, and prepare their heart unto thee"* [I Chronicles 29:18] and *"....for the LORD searcheth all hearts, and understandeth all the* imaginations *of the thoughts: if thou seek him, he will be found of thee; but if thou forsake him, he will cast thee off for ever"* [I Chronicles 28:9d-i]). In the rest of those scriptures, the words have very negative connotations, such as *hagah* ("the people imagine a vain thing") or *machashabah* ("wicked imaginations"), and others. This could be because, as Paul says, *"For I know that in me (that is, in my flesh,) dwelleth no good thing..."* (Romans 7:18 a-b).

COUNTERPOINT TO DISCUSSION POINT 1:
When We Become Saved, Our Mind Is Renewed; Once this Happens, We Immediately Imagine what God Imagines.

Proponents of imagination say that the fact that imagination is generated in the Believer's mind is not an issue because, once we become saved, our minds are renewed. To support this belief, they cite Romans 12:2, which says the following:

> *And be not conformed to this world: but be ye transformed by the renewing of your mind, that ye may prove what [is] that good, and acceptable, and perfect, will of God.*

Philippians 2: 5-6 is also quoted and it says the following:

Let this mind be in you, which was also in Christ Jesus:

Who, being in the form of God, thought it not robbery to be equal with God:

People who cite these scriptures in defense of imagination and the role it supposedly plays in creativity say that because the mind is renewed, we then take on the Mind of Christ. Therefore, they say, whatever we think must be what Christ thinks. And, from there, we can imagine whatever we want because our thinking has lined up with Christ's thinking and whatever we create from our thinking at that point is something that Christ gave us the power and the right to create.

Proponents of imagination would probably also say that once the mind is renewed that it does not rely on earthly prior knowledge, but, that instead, the mind has become that of Christ and is linked to the "wisdom of the ages", so that it relies on prior knowledge, context clues and inferences gained since the foundation of the earth (because God was here before the earth was formed.

COUNTER TO THE COUNTERPOINT TO DISCUSSION POINT 1: Renewal of the Mind is a Process.

I am in full agreement with Romans 12:2 and Philippians 2:5-6 and the fact that our goal as born again Christians is to be transformed and to have our minds renewed. But, I believe that we must interpret these scripture correctly. Specifically, we have to understand that the renewing of the mind/taking on the mind of Christ involves **submission** and **process**.

Romans 12:2 and Philippians 2:5-6 begin with "**Be ye**" and "**Let this**". Be and let are verbs that, in these contexts, denote that the person must ***become*** (be ye) or ***allow*** (let this). In other words, the person must ***allow*** the change to take place in his or her mind. ***There is an act of submission that has to take place.*** The person must realize that his or her mind is not pleasing to God and must make a conscious decision to allow God to change it. God does not violate our will (*"Behold, I stand at the door, and knock: if any man hear my voice, and open the door, I will come in to him, and will sup with him, and he with me"* [Revelations 3:20]) and will not force the change on us. He may allow situations to come that are intended to persuade us to yield our will to His Will, but He does not force anything on us; it is a conscious choice we have to make. If we have not submitted to the Lord, we will not receive the new mind. ***Submission is a process.***

Additionally, Romans 12:2 says "Be ye **transformed** by the **renewing** of your mind." Again, ***transformed*** and ***renewing*** are verbs that denote action. ***Transforming*** and ***renewing*** are both ***processes***.

The problem with suggesting that imagination is perfected immediately when we become saved because our minds are instantly renewed is that submission, transforming, renewing and processes associated with them are not taken into account. One can be saved, but if one is not completely yielded to God in a particular area, then one is not submitted to God in that area. And if one is not submitted to God in an area, that area cannot be perfected. Even if one is submitted to God in an area, the submission, transforming and renewing are processes. And, processes take time!

We are so fearfully and wonderfully made by God (Psalms 139:14). Like a precious gemstone, we are multi-faceted. There are many components to us and many compartments to our minds. That being said, transforming and renewing take time. In fact, in some ways, it is a lifelong process. It involves the continual killing off of the old (carnal) mind so that the transformed person with the renewed mind can come forth. The Apostle Paul understood this daily process of submitting to God on a daily basis so that the carnal mind when he said, *"I protest by your rejoicing which I have in Christ Jesus our Lord, I die daily"* (I Corinthians 15:31).

Knowing this, how can one say, then, "how much" of his or her mind has been renewed versus how much has yet to be renewed? As this pertains to imagination, ***how*** do you know that the imaginations are coming out of the "renewed" portion of the mind versus "un-renewed" portions of the mind? We will discuss evil imaginations later in the chapter, but, outside of known evil imaginations, how does one know if what he or she is imagining and creating based on those imaginations actually lines up with what God's Will is for them to create?

Discussion Point 2:
Imagination is not necessarily the same as seeing or hearing in the Spirit and therefore may be unnecessary.

In the research I found on the role of the imagination in the Christian life, I found a common theme. I discovered that many people had a habit of saying that they "imagined" things that the Holy Spirit had, in fact, revealed to them. To the point, they would take credit for certain ideas or creativity being a result of "their imagination" rather than a result of them being obedient and causing to come to pass the things that God had spoken to them, showed them, or that the Holy Spirit directed them to do. I know that people may use the word,

"I imagined" or, "I saw in my mind's eye" to denote something that is really something that God showed them or the Holy Spirit revealed to them. But, they are not the same thing.

To further research the point that hearing and seeing in the spirit are not the same as imagining something, I had discussions with various groups of ministers. In the discussions, I asked them what is the difference between God showing them something or telling them something versus them imagining it. As you will read in the counterpoint, their response was one that almost stymied me, for several reasons. I could not understand how people could take credit for "imagining" the things that God had spoken to them. Likewise, it seemed just to make sense to me that, if God shows or tells me something, I don't have to "imagine" it. This is true of any creative endeavor that He wants me to do.

For instance, if I am looking at television (my set is on, reception is good, volume is appropriate), I don't have to "imagine" what the characters look like, what they sound like or what they are doing. If I have watched the program from the beginning to the end, I know the characters' names, the setting, the plots and subplots, the conflicts, the resolutions to the conflicts, and even the wardrobe! Now, once the program ends, I may imagine what the characters would do next, etc., but I do not have to use "*the faculty or action of forming new ideas, or images or concepts of external objects* ***not present to the senses***". This is because the characters and their voices ***were*** present to my senses; I could ***see*** them on the screen. I could ***hear*** their voices. I can ***discern*** the plot and conflicts and ***remember*** the resolution of the conflicts and ***recall*** the wardrobe. Now, if the program is a two-part episode, I don't even have to 'imagine" what the next episode will bring. If I ***stay tuned*** and be in the right place at the right time when the next episode comes on, I can watch it and get the information.

God said the reason a lot of Christians rely on imagination to create things is that they don't ***stay tuned***. He said that they stay still long enough to get a little portion of the revelation that He is trying to impart to them about what He wants them to do, make or create. Then, they either get excited or impatient and they take off on their own without getting the rest of the story. Some people have started off to write books but have gotten impatient and have either given up or wrote the book out of their fleshly thinking; they did not wait on the revelation of God. There are people who God has promised a successful singing and songwriting career. He blesses them to write and record a few songs. But, when success does not happen in their own timing, they turn to their ***own imaginations*** and either give up, stop writing, or begin to write, sing and record songs based on what they think will "sell". God said they have, in fact, sold out. They have silenced the gifting or calling He placed in them because they will not "broadcast" what He is sending through them. They are getting their signals crossed (with God and imagination). And, crossed signals cause static, both in the physical realm and in the spiritual realm! ***God said if we learn to see what God is showing us, hear what He is saying to us, and discern what He is doing, there is no need to "imagine."***

COUNTERPOINT TO DISCUSSION POINT 2:

"You are a prophet, and God only speaks to you and other prophetic people like that. The non-prophetic people don't hear God like you and have to rely on their imagination."

Readers, the above comment—a composite of a couple of direct quotes spoken by well-meaning Men and Women of God with whom I broached the subject of imagination and its role in the Christian life - is the comment that nearly stymied me! Granted, I understand that there are different gifts and different diversities of gifts (I Corinthians 12:4). I also understand that there are also different callings (I Corinthians 12:28), and that everyone is not called like I am to the Office of the Prophet. But, it never occurred to me that there are people who either do not aspire to hear or see in the Spirit because they feel they are not supposed to do so based on their calling. Nor did it occur to me that there are people who have a relationship with the Lord who do not hear Him speak or to whom He does not show them things. And, to think that because people do not hear Him and therefore have to rely on their imagination to do things was unfathomable to me.

COUNTER TO COUNTERPOINT #2:
God is no Respecter of Persons; He Speaks to Each of Us in His/Our Own Way.

The Bible says that My (God's) sheep know my voice (John 10:27). "***MY SHEEP,***" the scripture says. It does not say "my **prophetic** sheep" or "my sheep w**ho are called to the office of the prophet**." It says, "**my sheep**." Granted, there may be a different/deeper level of seeing for those who have the gift of prophecy or those who are called to the Office of the Prophet, but God knows that we have to live here on earth, walk out our callings and giftings, fight the enemy…He would not have us to do all of this without having access to His "Input"; *He gives His Input by speaking to us and/or showing us what He would want us to do*. The same is true about being creative; ***He would not just leave it up to our imaginations for us to birth whatever it is He is wanting us to birth in the earth realm.***

Speak, Lord, Speak

God showed me that, in the Bible, whenever He wanted something created in the earth realm, He either **spoke** to someone, **showed** them something or **placed** something in their spirit to let them know that it was His Will/His Mandate for them to create whatever it was and then gave them instructions as to how to go about it. When God wanted the Ark built, He **spoke** to Noah and **gave him instructions** as to what type of wood to use, the specifications and what animals to put in it (Genesis 6:14). When God wanted Abram to "create" the lineage of Jesus, God **spoke** to Abram and **told** him to ***"... Get thee out of thy country, and from thy kindred, and from thy father's house, unto a land that I will*** **shew** ***thee***" (Genesis 12:1). When it was time for the Temple to be built, God **spoke** to David but **gave specific instructions** (blueprints) to Solomon (I Kings 3:16). When trying to get Jacob's attention, God **allowed** Jacob **to have a dream** (Genesis 28:10-22) and then **allowed him to wrestle with the angel**. He **spoke** to Moses **through the burning bush** (Exodus 3:1-15). He **spoke** to Balaam **through the donkey** (Numbers 22). And He **spoke** to the New Testament Saul by **blinding him with the bright light** (Acts 13:9). He **spoke** to the Apostles **through the deaths of Ananias and Sapphira.** (Acts 5:1-11)

Each person has his or her own Divinely engineered creative process. Different creative people say that different things inspire them to create. This is because God speaks to artists/creators **differently**. Some creative people receive inspiration by taking walks in the park; they gain insight being quiet and listening. Some creative people work best at night, while others work best in the mornings. Some people are inspired by dreams. I have heard it said that musicians or songwriters might just hear a tune in their spirit and begin to create the songs. As a writer, I can hear what to write in my spirit. While I am hearing, I type what I am hearing onto the page in a Microsoft Word document. I do not type for accuracy; I type it as fast as I can get it out. Then, I go back and edit for typos later. Sometimes, I have to take a break and walk around. Then I come back to typing. I do this until God tells me I am finished for that day or night.

Creative people have been known to be very fickle, hence the term *temperamental artists*. Usually, a temperamental artist has to have just the right atmosphere to receive creative inspirations; these atmospheric conditions tend to result in what most people would think to be a strange attitude on the part of the artist. Nevertheless, it is under these conditions that the artist/creative person flourishes. With each type of artist/creative person, he or she has different ways in which he or she hears God give this inspiration. The creative people themselves are not ***imagining*** that they are being inspired; ***they are receiving inspiration from God***, but they are receiving it in their own unique way that God speaks to them.

On the other hand, God is not pleased with creations that come solely out of the imagination of man. At the tower of Babel, God had to send different languages upon the people because the people were using their ***"own imaginations"*** to try to create a tower that would reach all the way up to heaven. The passage is as follows:

> *And the whole earth was of one language, and of one speech.*
>
> *And it came to pass, as they journeyed from the east, that they found a plain in the land of Shinar; and they dwelt there.*

And they said one to another, Go to, let us make brick, and burn them throughly. And they had brick for stone, and slime had they for morter.

And they said, Go to, let us build us a city and a tower, whose top may reach unto heaven; and let us make us a name, lest we be scattered abroad upon the face of the whole earth.

And the LORD came down to see the city and the tower, which the children of men builded.

And the LORD said, Behold, the people is one, and they have all one language; and this they begin to do: and now nothing will be restrained from them, which they have **imagined** *to do.*

Go to, let us go down, and there confound their language, that they may not understand one another's speech.

So the LORD scattered them abroad from thence upon the face of all the earth: and they left off to build the city.

Therefore is the name of it called Babel; because the LORD did there confound the language of all the earth: and from thence did the LORD scatter them abroad upon the face of all the earth. **– Genesis 11:1-9**

Imagination can in no way replace the Voice of God speaking directly to our spirits or Him giving Divine Instruction in showing us something. In fact, I believe that if we hear Him or understand what He is saying to us, there is no need to imagine. While I will admit that perhaps other people whose spiritual vision is not as keen as mine is as a prophet may have difficulty seeing as hearing as clearly as I do, I do not think that anyone should supplement spiritual hearing, seeing or perception with using their own imagination. I believe that whatever God wants to birth through a person via the person's creativity God will give the person instructions in the special way that God speaks to that particular person.

Imagination in this sense then, ***may silence a gifting or calling because the person doing the imagining no longer relies on what God is leading them to do*** (showing, telling), but begins to lean to their own understanding. The Bible expressly forbids this (Proverbs 3:5). When this happens, the person moves in his or her own strength. The work to be done then is done in the flesh without spiritual guidance from the Holy Spirit. And, when that happens, the person is no longer walking in his or her spiritual gifting or calling. The person has been lulled into a false sense of security by the enemy and is now listening to the flesh rather than listening to God.

Semantics: Imagination versus Imaging

I understand that words in our English language can have several meanings, connotations and syntaxes. In writing this chapter, I made a conscious effort to not interpret the word ***imagination*** as something that is strictly fantasy or make-believe (even though that is one of the definitions at the beginning of this chapter for the word *imagine)*. For instance, an *imaginary friend* is one that has been created in the *imagination* of a person (usually a child). The imaginary friend does not exist in reality and often thought of as not real. In this context then, imagination would produce pure fantasy. While I am not sure that I fully accept that imagination is necessary for creativity, I am not prepared at this point to relegate imagination to the context of being completely not real or able to produce anything tangible.

In fact, I think that it is possible that when most Christians use the term *imagination* in terms of being able to see what God has commanded them to create or do, they really do not know the definition of *imagination*, but need to call the process "**something**." I would suggest that, instead of saying we are **imagining** something, we say our brain/mind is **imaging** what God is speaking to us or showing us to do. I am thinking of terms of medical imaging equipment that detects when something is in its scope and produces an image of it. This way, we are saying that we are reflecting what God is showing/projecting. We are not taking any credit for (i.e., "***my imagination***"), nor are we discrediting the **reality** of God speaking to us.

Ungodly Imaginations

To this point, I have written about imagination and its perceived role in creativity. While I may not have found many sources with whom I completely agreed as to the role of imagination, I agreed with most sources about the dangers of ungodly imaginations. As I said earlier, out of the 36 instances of the word *imagination* or *imagine* being listed in some form in the Bible, only two of those instances show imagination in a possible non-ungodly light. The rest of the scriptures show imagination to be something that is ungodly; it is shown as vain, wicked, and from the hearts of vain and wicked men. Some of those scriptures are shown below:

> *Thou hast seen all their vengeance and all their **imaginations** against me.*

Thou hast heard their reproach, O LORD, and all their **imaginations** *against me.* – **Lamentations 3:60-61**

For the wrath of God is revealed from heaven against all ungodliness and unrighteousness of men, who hold the truth in unrighteousness;

Because that which may be known of God is manifest in them; for God hath shewed it unto them.

For the invisible things of him from the creation of the world are clearly seen, being understood by the things that are made, even his eternal power and Godhead; so that they are without excuse:

Because that, when they knew God, they glorified him not as God, neither were thankful; but became vain in their **imaginations**, *and their foolish heart was darkened.*
– **Romans 1:18-21**

Casting down **imaginations**, *and every high thing that exalteth itself against the knowledge of God, and bringing into captivity every thought to the obedience of Christ*
– **II Corinthians 10:5**

Why do the heathen rage, and the people **imagine** *a vain thing?* – **Psalms 2:1**

Deceit is *in the heart of them that* **imagine** *evil: but to the counsellors of peace* is *joy.* – **Proverbs 12:20**

For they intended evil against thee: they **imagined** *a mischievous device,* which *they are not able* to perform.
– **Psalms 21:11**

When our imaginations are ungodly - vain and evil - we have yielded our minds to Satan. We as Christians must be so careful as to what we entertain in our minds. If we are not careful, ungodly imaginations take root and become ungodly fruits in our lives. Those ungodly fruits become ungodly actions. The Bible says that we cannot serve both God and Mammon (Matthew 6:24). If we entertain ungodly imaginations, we risk silencing our gifting or calling because we are in effect giving more of a voice to the enemy than we are to God.

SYNOPSIS

In some ways, imagination can serve to silence our giftings and callings. It can do that by causing the mind to be focused on what a person's perceived "own" abilities are, rather than the abilities in Christ. Our giftings and callings can also be silenced by imagination when we rely more on what we are imagining versus what God has shown us to do; we have to learn how to hear how God speaks to us as individuals, home in on that and glean instruction from that. Finally, we must guard our hearts against evil imaginations, being careful not to align ourselves with the thinking, plots and plans of the enemy. If we do not, we stand a good chance of operating (albeit unwittingly sometimes) in the kingdom of darkness and not fulfilling the mandates that God has placed upon our lives.

L

Little Foxes

God showed me that often in our walk with the Lord, we concentrate on what we perceive to be the "big, important" things. We don't murder (Exodus 20:13), neither do we commit adultery (Exodus 20:14) nor commit any of the sins that we consider definite "no no's". We love the Lord with our whole hearts. We strive to do what pleases Him and what edifies the Kingdom. And, yet, He said, we "hermitia" - we *miss the mark*. Make no mistake, when we miss the mark, we sin. And, we do so by neglecting what seem to be the "little things". We let these "little things" keep us from walking in the fullness of what God would have for us and from enjoying the fruits of living a Holy life. Song of Solomon 2:15 says it in the following manner:

> *Take us the foxes, the little foxes, that spoil the vines: for our vines* have *tender grapes.*

The term *little foxes* in this scripture comes from the Hebrew word *shuw`al*. This word was actually be used to denote jackals as well. In Biblical days, Jackals were thought of as glorified wild canines (wild dogs). My husband Ron is an avid animal lover and, unlike me, knows much about all kinds of wildlife. He said that it would not be a stretch to assume that the *little foxes* in the scripture were actually jackals. This, he said, is because jackals are more opportunistic than foxes. Foxes like to hunt for small prey; Jackals will hunt, too, but are more apt to take the opportunity of eating grapes that are readily available to them. So, when we speak of *little foxes* for the rest of this chapter, we will really be thinking of ***little jackals***.

Grapes are fruits. And, we are to bear fruit. Regarding bearing fruit, the Matthew 7:15-20 says the following:

> *Beware of false prophets, which come to you in sheep's clothing, but inwardly they are ravening wolves.*
>
> *Ye shall know them by their* **fruits**. *Do men gather grapes of thorns, or figs of thistles?*
>
> *Even so every good tree bringeth forth good* **fruit**; *but a corrupt tree bringeth forth evil* **fruit**.
>
> *A good tree cannot bring forth evil* **fruit**, *neither can a corrupt tree bring forth good* **fruit**.
>
> *Every tree that bringeth not forth good* **fruit** *is hewn down, and cast into the fire.*
>
> *Wherefore by their* **fruits** *ye shall know them.*

So, then, when we allow the *little foxes* (*shuw`al;* **little *jackals; wild dogs***) to get our grapes off our vines, we have, in essence, allowed our fruits to go to the dogs! We are allowing our giftings and callings to be silenced.

When praying about what the subject matter of this chapter would be, I originally thought that this chapter would be an in-depth study of the differences between sins, iniquities, and transgressions. Perhaps I will include that information in another book in some form, but, God said, that we are missing the mark in "little" areas and that He wanted me to use this chapter to address those areas.

This missing the mark is causing us to not walk in the completeness of Him.

Little Foxes are not Cute!

As God was giving me the layout for this chapter (at this time, I am the author, designer, publisher and sometimes proofreader, so that I not only write the content, but I design the pages and the cover as well), I remembered this animal shapes font I have. I downloaded this font months ago, not knowing why, because it is not one I would use typically. However, I felt led of the Lord to download the font, and I did. Today it became rhema to me why God instructed me to get this font: ***It was for this very chapter.*** Again, not knowing much about animals, I asked Ron to go through the animal characters in the font and choose which one(s) would most accurately symbolize the *little foxes* in this chapter (I know what a fox looks like, but, admittedly, I could not pick out the silhouette of the jackal or even discern if any of the animal silhouettes would be that of a jackal). He did. As it turned out, there was in fact a silhouette for both a fox and a jackal. I was inclined to use the fox silhouette, because it was "cuter"; it has a fluffy tail and looked "cuddlier" than did the jackal. In fact, the jackal's silhouette was, well, **kind of scary**! So I started using the fox silhouette.

But, then the Lord jolted me. He told me, "Don't use the fox! Use the silhouette of the jackal!" "Uh oh!", I thought. I felt like I was in trouble with Him. He further said, "That is the problem now!" I instantly understood what He was saying: ***Sin looks too "cute" and "cuddly" to us***. It should not! We think, "The *little foxes* look 'alright'; what's the harm?" The harm is that it is still **sin**! And, it is **sin** - in all its forms ("big" and little") - that **separates us from Him** (Isaiah 59:2). Sin is **ugly** to Him. It is **[sin]ister**. **It is a stench**

in His Nostrils! I repented and began to use the semiotic of the jackal that you will read about below. There are five jackal examples. Each jackal will be used to denote a *little fox*.

(LITTLE) WHITE LIES/FIBS

White lies/fibs is the first of the *little foxes* God led me to discuss. It is quite common for people in the Body of Christ who would not dream of telling a "real lie" to have no qualms about "fibbing" or telling what has come to be known as a white lie. By terming it a "white" lie, it seems to soften the impact of the fact that the statement made was false, or a lie. In the scriptures white is used to denote purity and cleanliness ("*These are they which came out of great tribulation, and have washed their robes, and made them white in the blood of the Lamb*" [Revelation 7:14d-f]), but in reality, there is nothing pure or clean about a lie.

Partial truths, exaggerations and even some excuses are lies; that's all there is to it! To call them little white lies and fibs is further perpetuating the lies - when we do that, we are then lying about the lies!

Most little white lies and fibs could be eliminated if we would take heed to Matthew 5:37 which says the following:

> *But let your communication be, Yea, yea; Nay, nay: for whatsoever is more than these cometh of evil.*

In other words, if you **can** do something and you **want** to do something, then, when someone asks you to do it, say yes. But, if you **can't** do something (if you are too busy, don't have the time, energy or the money to do it) or you **don't want** to do something, then, say no when asked to do it. If you can't pay a bill at that moment, then say so and/or don't say you will pay it when you know you won't. If you don't like something, don't lie and say that you do. Many white lies or fibs are told to impress man, to keep from hurting man's feelings, or to keep man from thinking badly of us. But, when we opt to tell a white lie or a fib, we are putting man's feelings and his opinion of us in a higher place than we are putting God's consideration of the matter and His judgment of us. We would rather please man by telling a lie and risk hurting God (because when we sin, we crucify Christ afresh [Hebrews 6:6]). We also risk an eternity out of the presence of the Lord, because the Bible says that all liars will have their part in the lake of fire (Revelations 21:8).

In Chapter S: Scared, we read about Abram who told the white lie of Sarai being his sister to escape harm at the hands of the Pharaoh (Genesis 12). We discussed the possible far-reaching implications that that one lie could have had had it not been revealed to Pharaoh that he was being duped. It could have cost mankind a Savior. Likewise, our white lies have implications, too.

With each white lie we tell, we align ourselves with Satan, "the father of lies" (John 8:44). When we speak lies, we are opening ourselves up to speak out of the kingdom of darkness, which means that we are closing ourselves off from receiving revelation from God. When that happens, our giftings and callings get silenced.

FAILURE TO MAINTAIN A CONSISTENT PRAYER LIFE

Lackadaisicalness opens the door for many *little foxes*. This is particularly true in the area of being haphazardly disobedient. Disobedience to God is a sin, whether it is done deliberately or haphazardly. In fact, it can be argued that all sin is disobedience to the laws of God. And, there is no substitute for obedience. In fact, I Samuel 15:22 says the following:

> *And Samuel said, Hath the LORD* as great *delight in burnt offerings and sacrifices, as in obeying the voice of the LORD? Behold,* **to obey** *is* **better than sacrifice**, and *to hearken than the fat of rams.*

We tend to hear and obey God if He says for us to minister to someone, to give a prophetic word, or to do something that involves ministering to others. But, when it comes to the following areas, the *little fox* of haphazard disobedience comes to steal our fruit and the enemy to wreak havoc in our spiritual lives: ***Failure to maintain a consistent prayer life, failure to maintain a consistent praise and worship regimen*** and ***failure to read the Bible and study the Word regularly***.

Many Christians are lax in maintaining a regular prayer life. When God commands them to get up at a certain time of the morning and pray, they convince themselves that they have prayed enough the night before or that they can do it later, but later never comes. Or, when God says to turn off the television, get off the Internet, shut down the iPod or stop whatever activity they are doing at the time and enter into prayer, many Christians dismiss the Voice of God. But, prayer is crucial to the life of the Believer. Daniel prayed three times a day (Daniel 6:10). Prayer was so essential to effective Kingdom living until Jesus left us what has come to be known as The Lord's Prayer, a paradigm for a successful prayer (Matthew 6:9-13).

Prayer is the means of communication between the Believer and God the Father (Philemon 4:6). Prayer is also a means of receiving Divine Instruction. Through prayer, we can tear down strongholds in the spirit realm (James 5:16). Miracles are wrought (I Samuel 1:1-2:11), healings take place (James 5:15), supernatural increase manifests

(Matthew 14:15) - all through prayer. It is no wonder then, that enemy would bring a spirit of lackadaisicalness to us to cause us to be haphazardly disobedient in the area of maintaining a regular prayer life. When we are not praying, we are not receiving instruction. And, when we are not receiving instruction, we have no Word to give to the people. And, when we have no Word to give to the people, our prophetic gifting and calling has been silenced.

FAILURE TO MAINTAIN A CONSISTENT PRAISE AND WORSHIP REGIMEN

Another area in which some Christians are lax is in the area of maintaining a regular praise and worship life. David loved to praise and worship. He danced before the Lord (II Samuel 6:14). David knew that it is through praise and worship that the relationship between God and man grows. Praise and worship establish and atmosphere in which the shekinah glory of God can come and rest upon us. This is the same glory cloud that was with Moses and the Children of Israel in their journey in the wilderness. It gave them guidance and light (Exodus 13:18-22). This *little fox* causes us to miss out on the glory of God in our lives when we do not praise and worship as we should.

FAILURE TO READ AND STUDY THE BIBLE REGULARLY

Psalms 119:105 declares that the Word of God is, "*a lamp unto my feet and a light unto my path*". II Timothy 2:15 tells us to, "*Study to shew thyself approved unto God, a workman that needeth not to be ashamed, rightly dividing the word of truth.*" Our spiritual lifeline is studying the Word of God ("*Search the scriptures; for in them ye think ye have eternal life: and they are they which testify of me*" [John 5:39]).

As the Children of God, we should take every opportunity that we can to get to know God and to know as much as about Him as we possibly can. There is no better way of doing this than by reading our Bibles and studying the Word of God. The Word of God is the Bread of Life (because Jesus is the Bread of Life [John 6:48] and Jesus is the Word [John 1:1]). It is rivers of living water (John 7:38). It is the milk and the strong meat (I Corinthians 3:2) of the spiritual diet. Just as the physical body cannot live without food and water for prolonged periods, so the spiritual being cannot live without the Word of God.

In the physical realm, children who suffer from malnutrition have a myriad of developmental problems including delayed cognitive functioning, stunted growth and various mental and emotional disorders. Likewise, when we as the Children of God neglect to eat of His Word and eat on a consistent and timely basis, we stunt our spiritual growth and open the door for a myriad of dysfunctions in our spiritual growth. We cannot properly walk in our gifting or callings if we do not read our Bibles and study the Word of God consistently.

ALLOWING JUNK INTO OUR SPIRITS

We have to be careful that while we enjoy our spiritual freedom and freedom from the law and religion, we do not allow junk into our spirits. Junk includes ungodly words, thoughts, images or ideas. These things can get into our spirits by things that we watch (television, movies, plays), see (pictures, actions), read (books, letters, emails, chats, blogs) or hear (conversations and music).

Regarding allowing junk into our spirits through what we hear and what we watch, the Bible says the following:

> *Only let your conversation be as it becometh the gospel of Christ: that whether I come and see you, or else be absent,*

I may hear of your affairs, that ye stand fast in one spirit, with one mind striving together for the faith of the gospel.
– Philippians 1:27

I will set no wicked thing before mine eyes: I hate the work of them that turn aside; it *shall not cleave to me.*
– Psalms 101:3

Listening to gossip, hearing jokes with profanity or hearing anything with questionable content may be a gateway to the enemy infiltrating our spirits. We as Believers may not be offended by what we hear, nor we may not see an immediate effect of hearing these things, but, if we saturate our spirits with junk (especially if we are not taking the time to pray, to praise and worship and to read our Bibles), it is sure to produce unsavory results. In planting, what you put into the ground is what you get out of it. If a seed of junk has been planted and cultivated instead of a seed of righteousness, a junk mentality will grow, instead of a tree of righteousness (Matthew 12:33). The gifts and calling of God are without repentance (Romans 11:29), but in order to bring forth those giftings and callings into spiritual maturity, we must have healthy spirits from which those giftings and callings can come forth. Junk produces an unhealthy spirit.

Little Foxes/A Little Leaven

Galatians 5:9 says, *"A little leaven leaveneth the whole lump."* Leaven is yeast. The idea is that a little yeast would cause the whole lump of dough to rise, an unwanted effect if the desired outcome is to make flat bread. The idea behind this proverb-like scripture is that a little sin will spoil the entire "body". In this way, a little leaven is like *little foxes*; both are used to show the destruction that sin –

even a little - can cause in the life of the Believer. The *little foxes* discussed in this chapter are but a few of the often-overlooked sins committed by Believers. It is in our best interests as Children of God to mind our grapes, taking inventory on a regular basis (I Corinthians 11:28). If we find ourselves missing the mark in any areas, we need only to confess and to repent and make a choice to not fall back into that area of sin again. We must keep the *little foxes* at bay so that our spiritual fruits can grow and flourish. Then, we can complete the Father's Divine Purpose for our lives.

Euroclydon

Who Has Seen the Wind?
By Christina Rossetti

Who has seen the wind?
Neither I nor you:
But when the leaves hang trembling,
The wind is passing through.

Who has seen the wind?
Neither you nor I:
But when the trees bow down their heads,
The wind is passing by.[2]

Euroclydon, which means "*northeasterner*", is a cyclonic northeastern windstorm that is common in the Mediterranean. In Acts 27 and Acts 28, Paul, while at sea, experiences such a storm. It changes his life forever and sets him even further on the path to destiny. Paul, acting under the direction of the Holy Spirit, makes it through the ordeal, coming out alive and victorious, and moving in a greater level of power and anointing than ever before. He conquered the storm. But, in praying about the subject of this chapter, I heard in my spirit that the Euroclydon of our lives can sometimes wipe us out.

God said that a storm will either make us or break us. The storms that we go through are often allowed by God to prove us but used by the enemy to silence our giftings and callings. God said that storms will come, but how we deal with them and how prepared we are for them will make the difference in whether we are successful in walking out our callings.

The format of this chapter is as follows: The content of the chapter will be given in seven sections. Each section will contain a passage of scripture followed by a synopsis of the passage. Then, I will share a prophetic word that God has given me that corresponds with that particular portion of the story/the passage. This chapter will be different from most of the others I have written in that the emphasis will not necessarily be on teaching and explaining; it will be giving a prophetic word of wisdom or knowledge, as the Lord leads. God said that He wants His People to hear directly from Him regarding the storms that they have gone through, are currently going through and will go through in the future.

Because this content will be a Word of Wisdom or Word of Knowledge, although it may be written on one tense (past, present or future), it may or may not have happened already (i.e., one reader's past may be another reader's present or future). But, it is a word from God and it shall come to pass. He that that ears to hear let him hear what the Spirit would say to the church.

Section One: The Calm Before the Storm

Acts 26:1-26

1 Then Agrippa said unto Paul, Thou art permitted to speak for thyself. Then Paul stretched forth the hand, and answered for himself:

2 I think myself happy, king Agrippa, because I shall answer for myself this day before thee touching all the things whereof I am accused of the Jews:

3 Especially because I know thee to be expert in all customs and questions which are among the Jews: wherefore I beseech thee to hear me patiently.

4 My manner of life from my youth, which was at the first among mine own nation at Jerusalem, know all the Jews;

5 Which knew me from the beginning, if they would testify, that after the most straitest sect of our religion I lived a Pharisee.

6 And now I stand and am judged for the hope of the promise made of God unto our fathers:

7 Unto which promise our twelve tribes, instantly serving God day and night, hope to come. For which hope's sake, king Agrippa, I am accused of the Jews.

8 Why should it be thought a thing incredible with you, that God should raise the dead?

9 I verily thought with myself, that I ought to do many things contrary to the name of Jesus of Nazareth.

10 Which thing I also did in Jerusalem: and many of the saints did I shut up in prison, having received authority from the chief priests; and when they were put to death, I gave my voice against them.

11 And I punished them oft in every synagogue, and compelled them to blaspheme; and being exceedingly mad against them, I persecuted them even unto strange cities.

12 Whereupon as I went to Damascus with authority and commission from the chief priests,

13 At midday, O king, I saw in the way a light from heaven, above the brightness of the sun, shining round about me and them which journeyed with me.

14 And when we were all fallen to the earth, I heard a voice speaking unto me, and saying in the Hebrew tongue, Saul, Saul, why persecutest thou me? it is hard for thee to kick against the pricks.

15 And I said, Who art thou, Lord? And he said, I am Jesus whom thou persecutest.

16 But rise, and stand upon thy feet: for I have appeared unto thee for this purpose, to make thee a minister and a witness both of these things which thou hast seen, and of those things in the which I will appear unto thee;

17 Delivering thee from the people, and from the Gentiles, unto whom now I send thee,

18 To open their eyes, and to turn them from darkness to light, and from the power of Satan unto God, that they may receive forgiveness of sins, and inheritance among them which are sanctified by faith that is in me.

19 Whereupon, O king Agrippa, I was not disobedient unto the heavenly vision:

20 But shewed first unto them of Damascus, and at Jerusalem, and throughout all the coasts of Judaea, and then to the Gentiles, that they should repent and turn to God, and do works meet for repentance.

21 For these causes the Jews caught me in the temple, and went about to kill me.

22 Having therefore obtained help of God, I continue unto this day, witnessing both to small and great, saying none other things than those which the prophets and Moses did say should come:

23 That Christ should suffer, and that he should be the first that should rise from the dead, and should shew light unto the people, and to the Gentiles.

24 And as he thus spake for himself, Festus said with a loud voice, Paul, thou art beside thyself; much learning doth make thee mad.

25 But he said, I am not mad, most noble Festus; but speak forth the words of truth and soberness.

26 For the king knoweth of these things, before whom also I speak freely: for I am persuaded that none of these things are hidden from him; for this thing was not done in a corner.

Synopsis

Acts 26-28 tells the story of Paul being taken prisoner by King Agrippa and being sent on a ship to Rome with other prisoners. In Acts 26, Paul was questioned by King Agrippa. Paul gives his testimony of his conversion to Christianity. Festus, who was also present, thought that

Paul was insane or mentally unbalanced.

PROPHETIC WORD

Your testimony, your testimony! God said that He has allowed you to go through many trials and tribulations to perfect your testimony. You have not understood WHY the path that you have had to travel has seemed more difficult than that of others. You have not understood why the path that you have had to travel has had so many twists and turns, ups and downs, highs and lows, in and outs, goes and stops. God said that He allowed this to mold and make you into the person that He would have you to be. He said that He used to your "walk" even in the early stages of it, first to get your attention and then to minister to others. Your testimony was the precursor to your Euroclydon.

God said that He has had you in a season of sharing your testimony and you have wondered why you are giving so many "personal" details of your life to people, some of whom you don't even know. God said that this is because you have matured to the point where you are an open epistle, known and read of men. You have submitted to the Lord to the point where whatever you go through is mete for the Master's Use.

Because of the call that you have on your life, from the early days of your "introduction" to Christ, your walk has been "different", I hear the Lord say. God said that you are peculiar and have been since birth. He said He made you that way. You do not fit in with "the crowd" because He has made you unique and has called you out.
You have often been misunderstood. You have been called weird, crazy, and have been alienated, ridiculed and

rejected. You have been rejected by friends and loved ones. Those who you thought would be with you forever had turned and walked with you no more because of the stand that you have taken for Christ. Yes, even those who you served with in churches, who sat next to you on the pews, who sang in the choir/on the praise team with you, ministered side by side with you, stood as prayer partners/intercessors with and for you - they have not understood your stand for God and how He speaks to you and what He instructs you to do. You have experienced betrayal. They have left you and have rejected you in the process. But, God said that all of that was necessary to make you. All of that was necessary to cultivate you and condition you for the walk ahead. All of that was necessary to fortify you and solidify you for the journey that was to be your Spiritual Walk.

God said that He had to allow you to go through great trials and tribulations to press out of you all of the "substance" that He had put in you since before the foundations of the earth. It was through the heat and pressure of the fiery trials that you were proofed and perfected; it was through the heat and pressure of the fiery trials that you discovered what was inside of you. It was through the heat and pressure of the fiery trials that you discovered who God is in your life and who you are in the Kingdom of God. And, it is through the heat and pressure of the fiery trials that your testimony was perfected. But, that time and season of perfecting your testimony was for the walk to come.

God said too often people give up after or during the perfecting and proving time. They do not allow Him to use what they have gone through to take them into His Manifested Destiny for their lives. And because of this, they are not prepared for the storms. They are not prepared for the Euroclydon that will surely come.

Section Two: THROWN OVERBOARD

Acts 26: 27-32

27 King Agrippa, believest thou the prophets? I know that thou believest.

28 Then Agrippa said unto Paul, Almost thou persuadest me to be a Christian.

29 And Paul said, I would to God, that not only thou, but also all that hear me this day, were both almost, and altogether such as I am, except these bonds.

30 And when he had thus spoken, the king rose up, and the governor, and Bernice, and they that sat with them:

31 And when they were gone aside, they talked between themselves, saying, This man doeth nothing worthy of death or of bonds.

32 Then said Agrippa unto Festus, This man might have been set at liberty, if he had not appealed unto Caesar.

Synopsis

Paul's unwavering testimony about the goodness of Jesus Christ caused Agrippa to ponder salvation in his heart. The apostolic mantle on Paul's life was such that he felt an unction to present his case to the leaders of the land;

the government of the time. No other charge worthy of imprisonment was brought against Paul except "appealing to Caesar."

PROPHETIC WORD

God said that many in the Body will go through a season of being accused. There will be false accusations that will come by way of those close to you and those in authority. There will also be accusations that, while not false, will be brought because your stand for righteousness that you will take and your godly actions which will go against the will of the powers-that-be. As a result, people in authority will bring accusations against you. God said that the accusations became the precursor for the storm. He also said that how you handle the accusations will determine how you handle the storm.

God said in this season things that seem to be from the enemy will actually be from Him and that He will allow accusations and persecutions of the saints to manifest His Will in the earth realm. He said that at times He may choose to allow His Saints to be the sacrificial lamb, even as His Son Jesus was the sacrificial lamb. He said that He may also allow his saints to be persecuted because He is bringing judgment to the persecutors. He may also allow this to put his people in the right places at the right time to bring forth His Will in the earth realm.

God said that we must we willing and yielded to Him to serve in whatever capacity He chooses for our lives. Too often, He said, we want to be the mouthpieces of God, but we do not want to be the uncomely parts. He said we do not want to suffer. We must develop a mentality of suffering with Him for to suffer with Him is to reign with

Him. God said that we must love Him so much until we are willing to give our lives in service to Him. We must trust Him so much and have so much faith in Him until we know that we know that we know that when He tells us to do something, whatever the consequences are from man, the reward from Him is greater and more important.

It is through your righteous suffering that many will be led and won to the Lord. People will see the unwavering stance that you have taken for the Kingdom and for righteousness and will be pricked in their spirit and in their hearts to give the lives unto the Lord. Many people - some that you know and some that you do not know - are watching you and your walk with the Lord. They are listening to your "voice"; they are hearing what you are saying by your walk and your life. Are you willing to suffer for the sake of the Gospel? Are you willing to suffer for the advance of the Kingdom? Are you willing to let your voice be heard even if you have to suffer to do so?

In this season, being completely obedient and sold out to Him is key if we are going to walk in our calling and spiritual vocations.

Section Three: Storm Watch

Acts 27:1-13

1 And when it was determined that we should sail into Italy, they delivered Paul and certain other prisoners unto one named Julius, a centurion of Augustus' band.

2 And entering into a ship of **Adramyttium**, *we launched, meaning to sail by the coasts of Asia; one Aristarchus, a Macedonian of Thessalonica, being with us.*

3 And the next day we touched at Sidon. And Julius courteously entreated Paul, and gave him liberty to go unto his friends to refresh himself.

4 And when we had launched from thence, we sailed under Cyprus, because the winds were contrary.

5 And when we had sailed over the sea of Cilicia and Pamphylia, we came to Myra, a city of Lycia.

6 And there the centurion found a ship of Alexandria sailing into Italy; and he put us therein.

7 And when we had sailed slowly many days, and scarce were come over against Cnidus, the wind not suffering us, we sailed under Crete, over against Salmone;

8 And, hardly passing it, came unto a place which is called The fair havens; nigh whereunto was the city of Lasea.

9 Now when much time was spent, and when sailing was now dangerous, because the fast was now already past, Paul admonished them,
10 And said unto them, Sirs, I perceive that this voyage will be with hurt and much damage, not only of the lading and ship, but also of our lives.

11 Nevertheless the centurion believed the master and the owner of the ship, more than those things which were spoken by Paul.

12 And because the haven was not commodious to winter in, the more part advised to depart thence also, if by any means they might attain to Phenice, and there to winter; which is an haven of Crete, and lieth toward the south west and north west.

13 And when the south wind blew softly, supposing that they had obtained their purpose, loosing thence, they sailed close by Crete.

Synopsis

In Acts 27, Paul was put on a ship (the Adramyttium, whose name means, "*I shall abide in death*") with more than 200 other men (prisoners and sailors combined). Their destination was Italy. The centurion had great respect for Paul. Paul, having knowledge from the Holy Spirit, told the men on the ship that there was going to be trouble on the seas, but the men, including the centurion, did not take heed to Paul's warning.

PROPHETIC WORD

God has sent you with a Word (a solution) to help those around you. But they have not received you well. You know in your spirit that God has shown you something - has given you just what the people need - but they will not hear you. God said to tell you that the Word that He has given you is a sure word. He said that you are to not give up on what He has shown you. You are not to doubt or to allow a spirit of fear to creep in. The enemy will try to make you doubt who you are and what God has said to you. This, if successful, would serve to silence your gifting or calling. That is not the Will of the Lord for your life.

God said that because of all that you went through for your testimony, you are now "solid." He said that when others around you are dropping and falling by the wayside, you will stand. He said that even when you are in a situation in which you seem to have no control and it seems that your spiritual demise is sure, you will abide in death! Death may come nigh, but it will have to flee because of the calling that is on your life.

God said that He has been allowing you to gain favor with men in high places. Because of their position and their "mentality", they will not be able to receive all that you say at first, but their spirits will bear witness with the Spirit of God in you and in due time they will give their lives to the Lord. I will use even them to bring forth My expected, good end in your life.

Section Four: EUROCLYDON

Acts 27:14-26

14 But not long after there arose against it a tempestuous wind, called Euroclydon.

15 And when the ship was caught, and could not bear up into the wind, we let her drive.

16 And running under a certain island which is called Clauda, we had much work to come by the boat:

17 Which when they had taken up, they used helps, undergirding the ship; and, fearing lest they should fall into the quicksands, strake sail, and so were driven.

18 And we being exceedingly tossed with a tempest, the next day they lightened the ship;

19 And the third day we cast out with our own hands the tackling of the ship.

20 And when neither sun nor stars in many days appeared, and no small tempest lay on us, all hope that we should be saved was then taken away.

21 But after long abstinence Paul stood forth in the midst of them, and said, Sirs, ye should have hearkened unto me, and not have loosed from Crete, and to have gained this harm and loss.

22 And now I exhort you to be of good cheer: for there shall be no loss of any man's life among you, but of the ship.

23 For there stood by me this night the angel of God, whose I am, and whom I serve,

24 Saying, Fear not, Paul; thou must be brought before Caesar: and, lo, God hath given thee all them that sail with thee.

25 Wherefore, sirs, be of good cheer: for I believe God, that it shall be even as it was told me.

26 Howbeit we must be cast upon a certain island.

Synopsis

The Euroclydon hits. This is the same type of storm that hit when Jonah was in the boat and right before he was thrown overboard (Jonah 1:4). Paul's Euroclydon was one of great force and did much damage. Euroclydon are cyclonic storms, which mean that they continuously cycle for lengths of time. There was not much hope for survival. To lighten the load, Paul and the men had to throw some cargo overboard (this also parallels the story of Jonah because to lighten their "load" the men on Jonah's ship had to throw Jonah overboard [Jonah 1:15]).

Paul and the men had been hungry for many days. Paul told them that they should have listened to him at first regarding the Word he gave them about the storm. But, then he prophesied that no one would get hurt or die. He knew this because the night before an angel had visited him and told him this. Paul told them that they would get shipwrecked on an island.

PROPHETIC WORD

God said that you have or will go through a storm. It is unlike no other storm that you have ever gone through before. This storm is different. It is Euroclydon. This storm is different because it is a storm of wind; a storm of doctrine. This storm comes to shake you to your very core. It comes to make you question your very existence in God: "Did God really speak to you in the first place?", "Did I really hear what I thought I heard?", "Am I crazy?". It comes to bring deceptive thoughts; thoughts of depression, thoughts of suicide; thoughts of worthlessness and spiritual inferiority.

And, yet the Lord is allowing it because of this: If you withstand THIS storm, NOTHING will ever be able to shake you like this again! If you will go through Euroclydon and come out alive and well, there is nothing **else that Satan can throw at you that** will cause you to fall. Will he try after this to shake you? Yes. Will there be other storms? Yes. But, because of what you learn going through

Euroclydon, you will never be the same. Because of how you will learn to navigate through the "rough seas" and "strong winds", you will get your "sea legs". There will be nothing that the enemy will do that will cause you to falter after you go through this.

God said that during this season you will have to lighten the load. There have been some things that you have been carrying; some relationships, some burdens, some old guilts, some insecurities; some attitudes. There are some things that you have latched on to and there are some things that have attached themselves to you. In this season of storm, you will learn to recognize who and what you can live without. It is Euroclydon that will make plain to you what you have to do to get rid of these things. And, it is Euroclydon - or, rather, the will to get through it and get to the other side - that will give you the strength to get rid of these things, many of which you have learned to live with practically all of your life. Whenever you shed the weights, it will seem strange at first and it will seem strange to others around you because these things/relationships/people have been a part of what people have perceived that makes you "YOU" for a long time. But, you will throw .these things overboard with great ease because you will realize that the payoff for doing so means LIFE. And, the consequence for holding onto them could mean death. When you choose life over death, you will be choosing God over mammon/religion/tradition/flesh. It is because of this, you will grow into another dimension in the Spirit. You will come to lean on God to a greater degree than ever before. And, it will become rhema to you that God is all and nothing else matters. When this happens, you have chosen to cling to God and forsake everything and everyone else.

God said that there have been many who have gone through Euroclydon and, because of fear of the unknown, were too afraid to overthrow their cargo. When they did this, they made a god out of the things/relationships/attitudes to which they held on, and put those things in the place where He should be in their lives. Because of this, they did not withstand and have died spiritual deaths. Their callings and voices have been silenced. They may be physically alive, but spiritually, they are a shadow of their former selves. He that hath an ear to hear, let him hear.

God is saying, "I will give you instruction during the Euroclydon. You must be still - even with the strong winds, the rocking ship, the waves, the cries of fear of those around you - you must be still and listen. You must have faith in Me and in My ability and will to bring you out. You must have faith in who I have told you that you are in Me and know that I watch over My Word to perform it. You must know that I have begun a good work in you and am faithful to complete it. You must become ANCHORED IN ME even during the tumultuous times, when those around you have no visible means of help and when they are saying that it is over. I will use you and will use you mightily to speak My Words over the situation. I will use you mightily to speak in the midst of the storm. Men and women will look upon you and know that surely My hand is upon you because of the words that you speak and because they come to pass and not one falls to the ground. I will establish you as My True Mouthpiece in the land. But, you must be anchored in Me; you must be grounded in Me to receive My Word."

Section Five: WALKING IN YOUR AUTHORITY

Acts 27: 27-32

27 But when the fourteenth night was come, as we were driven up and down in Adria, about midnight the shipmen deemed that they drew near to some country;

28 And sounded, and found it twenty fathoms: and when they had gone a little further, they sounded again, and found it fifteen fathoms.

29 Then fearing lest we should have fallen upon rocks, they cast four anchors out of the stern, and wished for the day.

30 And as the shipmen were about to flee out of the ship, when they had let down the boat into the sea, under colour as though they would have cast anchors out of the foreship,

31 Paul said to the centurion and to the soldiers, Except these abide in the ship, ye cannot be saved.

32 Then the soldiers cut off the ropes of the boat, and let her fall off.

Synopsis

The storm kept going on and the crew went 14 days without eating. The crew measured the water and saw that the levels were getting less and less; the crew was afraid that the ship would run aground. The sailors, obviously forgetting what Paul said about no one getting hurt and/or not having in faith in what he said, tried to abandon the ship by lowering a smaller boat for the crew to use to escape; they were going to leave the prisoners to run aground on Adramyttium. Paul admonished them that if the crew and the commanding officers got off the original ship and escaped on the small boat, both they and the prisoners would die. So, the crew cut the ropes to the small boat, letting it go adrift, and stayed on the Adramyttium, per Paul's instructions.

Prophetic Word

There will come a time in the storm when you now master Euroclydon. The storm has not ended, nor have the physical attributes of the situation changed. But, YOU have changed. You have realized that this storm is allowed of God for your making. You have learned to find peace and fellowship with God in the midst of the storm. You have matured. You have found your voice and embraced your calling in the midst of the storm. You are walking in a greater level of spiritual authority than you ever have before.

At this point, God will increase your circle of influence. This is because God will use your ministry to serve as a witness to those who have been watching you and know that you are "for real." People - saved and unsaved - will see that your words do not fall to the ground. The unsaved will detect that there is something different about you and that the God that you serve is real. Because of this, they will be moved to obey God. They will do so because of the God that they see in you. You will have influence beyond the "logical" scope of your authority; but it will be Divinely orchestrated authority. God will get the glory out of all that you do. He will give you specific instructions that will save many alive - physically, spiritually, emotionally and psychologically. And, because you have allowed large parts of your carnality to die off in the storm, The Glory of the Lord can shine through you at a measure that has not been seen before. The Love of God and His Authority will shine through you, causing men who would not normally hear you and who do not normally receive instructions from the Lord to receive from you.

Section Six: Busted Boards & Broken Pieces

Acts 27:33-44

33 And while the day was coming on, Paul besought them all to take meat, saying, This day is the fourteenth day that ye have tarried and continued fasting, having taken nothing.

34 Wherefore I pray you to take some meat: for this is for your health: for there shall not an hair fall from the head of any of you.

35 And when he had thus spoken, he took bread, and gave thanks to God in presence of them all: and when he had broken it, he began to eat.

36 Then were they all of good cheer, and they also took some meat.

37 And we were in all in the ship two hundred threescore and sixteen souls.

38 And when they had eaten enough, they lightened the ship, and cast out the wheat into the sea.

39 And when it was day, they knew not the land: but they discovered a certain creek with a shore, into the which they were minded, if it were possible, to thrust in the ship.

40 And when they had taken up the anchors, they committed themselves unto the sea, and loosed the rudder bands, and hoised up the mainsail to the wind, and made toward shore.

41 And falling into a place where two seas met, they ran the ship aground; and the forepart stuck fast, and remained unmoveable, but the hinder part was broken with the violence of the waves.

42 And the soldiers' counsel was to kill the prisoners, lest any of them should swim out, and escape.

43 But the centurion, willing to save Paul, kept them from their purpose; and commanded that they which could swim should cast themselves first into the sea, and get to land:

44 And the rest, some on boards, and some on broken pieces of the ship. And so it came to pass, that they escaped all safe to land.

Synopsis

Paul begged all the men to eat something because they had not eaten in fourteen days, a very long time. He broke off a piece of bread, gave God praise for it and ate it. That encouraged them. All 276 who were on the boat then ate. The next morning, they saw a strange shoreline. They begin dropping anchor to dock. But, they hit a shoal and the boat began to come apart because the stern was being smashed by the waves. The sailors wanted to kill the prisoners so that when the prisoners got to the land, they would not escape. But, the centurion respected Paul and didn't want him or the others to get hurt. So, he thwarted the sailors' plans, ordering the prisoners to jump off the boat immediately and told them to grab whatever broken pieces of the boat that they could to hold on to. They did as he instructed and not one person was hurt or killed, just as Paul prophesied.

Prophetic Word

At the beginning of Euroclydon, there was much loss. You threw stuff overboard to survive and there was much damage done to your means of getting from one place to the next. Now you see the end in sight, but at what cost? God said that you will make it and will be used to help others that are going through something similar; others whose faith is not where yours is (because their calling is not what yours is). God said that you will instruct them how to come out of what you are coming out of, and that you will all come out victoriously.

At your word, people will make life-changing decisions but will do so with great ease because they trust the God in you. At this point, God will entrust you with an even greater level of responsibility. But, because He has already given you His Word on the situation, you will not experience burden of possibly not being right.

Both your faith in God's ability to provide and sustain and your faith in the creative power of God in YOU will cause you to be able to launch out into the deep on pieces and boards. Just as Jesus took the fish and loaves and caused them to multiply to feed the masses, you will tap into the supernatural power of God within you to use whatever you put your hands on - be it great or small - and it will be magnified and multiplied for Kingdom use. It will be perfected and primed for use by God. And, it will be an extension of your calling or gifting. People will marvel at what you are able to do with and make out of so little. God has given you just the right pieces and the right boards to get you to His Desired Destination for your life. You will masterfully navigate the rough, unsure waters (His Word that you do not have a complete revelation of for your life) to dry, safe land (your place of spiritual destiny and purpose).

Section Seven: For Such *a* Time as This

Acts 28:1-10

1 And when they were escaped, then they knew that the island was called Melita.

2 And the barbarous people shewed us no little kindness: for they kindled a fire, and received us every one, because of the present rain, and because of the cold.

3 And when Paul had gathered a bundle of sticks, and laid them on the fire, there came a viper out of the heat, and fastened on his hand.

4 And when the barbarians saw the venomous beast hang on his hand, they said among themselves, No doubt this man is a murderer, whom, though he hath escaped the sea, yet vengeance suffereth not to live.

5 And he shook off the beast into the fire, and felt no harm.

6 Howbeit they looked when he should have swollen, or fallen down dead suddenly: but after they had looked a great while, and saw no harm come to him, they changed their minds, and said that he was a god.

7 In the same quarters were possessions of the chief man of the island, whose name was Publius; who received us, and lodged us three days courteously.

8 And it came to pass, that the father of Publius lay sick of a fever and of a bloody flux: to whom Paul entered in, and prayed, and laid his hands on him, and healed him.

9 So when this was done, others also, which had diseases in the island, came, and were healed:

10 Who also honoured us with many honours; and when we departed, they laded us with such things as were necessary.

Synopsis

In Acts 28, the sailors and prisoners found out that the ship had wrecked on the island of Milita. It was rainy and cold there, so the people on the island were building a fire to help keep Paul and the others warm. To help with the fire, Paul began to pick up sticks to put on it. As he did so, a snake bit him and held on to his hand with its teeth. The people of Milita thought that since Paul was considered a prisoner, he must have been a murderer and that he was getting his "just desserts" by being bitten by the snake. They did not think he was going to make it; they thought the poisonous snakebite would kill him. But, Paul shook the snake off and kept going. They kept waiting for Paul to swell up or for some harm to come to him as a result of the snakebite, but he shook it off and kept going.

Shortly after that, Paul went to the house of Publius, the chief official of the island. His father was ill. Paul prayed for his father and his father was healed. The other people of the island who were sick also came and Paul prayed for them and they were healed. (Acts 28:9)

PROPHETIC WORD

God said, "When you come through Euroclydon, you will be empowered. You will walk in a greater level of anointing. You will see the Word manifested in your life as never before. Signs and wonders will follow you; YOU will be a sign and a wonder. Because this is often talked about, but not seen much in the earth realm, there will be some who will be unfamiliar with the way I move through you. They will wrongfully but not maliciously accuse you of operating out of your flesh or out of the realm of darkness. God said do not be moved by this but continue to move in Me and to move in love, for I am Love. It is through your love and through My hand continuously being on you that they will see Me in You and I will be glorified.

Whatever you put you hand to do, I will bless it in this season. This is because you will have My Mind and you will be thinking as I think. You will do as I would do. And, as you build fires - fires to illuminate people in my Word, fires to warm their frigid hearts, fires to purify them from all unrighteousness, fires to set them on the path to finding their own testimony and spiritual walk - I WILL BE THERE WITH YOU! I will be there with you. I will watch over My Word to perform it through you. "

I AM GRATEFUL FOR YOU

A Song by Destiny-Faith Hunt (Elizabeth Lenix)
Inspired by a Testimony of Prophetess O.W. Petcoff
May 24, 2010

I went through so many storms
Over the past year.
And sometimes I thought I would drown
'Cause I cried so many tears.
Although people encouraged me and
Said it would get better,
I thought the end was near.
That's when You stepped in and
All of my fears were gone.
Then I knew, it was with You, I belong.
You carried me through so many storms.
It's because of You, my life can move on.
And, I'm proud to tell everyone I know,
I am grateful for You. Oooh!
I am grateful for You Oooh!
I am grateful for You, Oooh!

---

[2]Rosetti, Christina. "Who Has Seen the Wind." *The Golden Book of Poetry*. Ed. Jane Werner. New York. Golden Press.

N

Nazareth

For the subject matter of this, the fifth chapter, the Lord spoke "Nazareth" to me and directed me to the passage of scripture below - John 1:43-49. It is as follows

The day following Jesus would go forth into Galilee, and findeth Philip, and saith unto him, Follow me.

Now Philip was of Bethsaida, the city of Andrew and Peter.

Philip findeth Nathanael, and saith unto him, We have found him, of whom Moses in the law, and the prophets, did write, Jesus of Nazareth, the son of Joseph.

And Nathanael said unto him, Can there any good thing come out of Nazareth? Philip saith unto him, Come and see.

Jesus saw Nathanael coming to him, and saith of him, Behold an Israelite indeed, in whom is no guile!

Nathanael saith unto him, Whence knowest thou me? Jesus answered and said unto him, Before that Philip called thee, when thou wast under the fig tree, I saw thee.

Nathanael answered and saith unto him, Rabbi, thou art the Son of God; thou art the King of Israel. **– John 1:43-49**

This passage begins with Jesus finding Philip and beckoning for Philip to follow Him and (eventually) become a disciple of Christ (John 1:43). Philip, excited about his new commission, began straightaway the task of finding others with whom he could share the Good News. He spots Nathanael and tells him that he is following Jesus, the fulfillment of Messianic prophecy (Micah 5:2). Nathanael, whose name means, *"Gift of God"*, knew of Jesus' presence but did not yet have a revelation of Who He really is. What he did know about Jesus, though, is that Jesus came from Nazareth, a town that, in Biblical days, had the reputation of being a small "one-horse" town with very little culture and very loose morals. Nathanael, not yet being spiritual minded, measured Jesus' ability to "be somebody" by where he came from and asked Phillip, "Can there any good thing come out of Nazareth?"(John 1:46)

God said that, in this passage of scripture and for His purposes for the chapter, Nazareth ***represents a bad and/or less-than-glamorous past—a reputation, a childhood, an "origin" which can cause shame or embarrassment.*** *Nazareth is an unsavory, unfavorable past.*

NAZARETH

Nazareth (whose name means, *"the guarded one"*) was the hometown of Jesus for 33 years of his life (Matthew 21:11). Nazareth was one of many small towns in the province of Galilee. In those days, Jerusalem, Judea and a few other surrounding cities were considered the cultural and commercial meccas of the area. The people of Jerusalem and Judea looked down upon the people of Galilee. Galilee was considered culturally deprived and behind the times. Galileans' speech was mocked and thought of as dowdy and improper. And, with many people of many different religions living in Galilee, it had the reputation of being amoral. In fact in Matthew 5:14 it is called, "*Galilee of the Gentiles.*" The reputation of Galilee was that it was not a preferred place to live.

While Galilee was looked down upon by Jerusalem and Judah, all the towns in Galilee looked down upon Nazareth. Of all the cities in Galilee, Nazareth was thought of as the worst of the worst. Within its walls were no large commercial ventures. In fact, except for a military post (a Roman garrison), there was not much else to see in Nazareth. And, up until the time of Jesus, while some well-known prophets or other people of influence had hailed from Galilee (Elisha, Barak and Gideon to name a few), Nazareth had not been home to any of them and could not use their fame to bolster its reputation.

Poor Nazareth! It just could not seem to catch a break! In addition to having the negative stigma of being in Galilee and being thought of as the worst of the worst by fellow Galileans, Nazareth was also a basin - a hole in the ground! And, it seemed that all of the exciting things that happened seemed to happen all around Nazareth, but not in Nazareth itself. A citation on Nazareth in the Unger Bible Dictionary says the following:

> "You cannot see from Nazareth the surrounding country, for Nazareth lies in a basin; but the moment you climb to the edge of this basin...what a view you have. Esdraelon lies before you, with its twenty battlefields - the scenes of Barak's and of Gideon's victories, of Saul's and Josiah's defeats, of the struggles for freedom in the glorious days of the Maccabees. There is Naboth's vineyard and the place of Jehu's revenge upon Jezebel; there is Shunem and the house of Elisha; there Carmel and the place of

> Elijah's sacrifice. To the east the valley of Jordan, with the long range of Gilead; to the west the radiance of the Great Sea…(Smith, Hist. Geog., p. 432)"[3]

No doubt, then, Nathanael grew up hearing the stereotypes about the people of Nazareth. He knew people from Nazareth were considered to be behind the times; he knew that they were thought of as not being able to speak properly; he knew that they were considered morally bankrupt. And, Nathanael who had probably grown up hearing all the stories (by Nathanael's time, these stories would have been centuries old) about famous Men of God and their exploits in surrounding cities, felt that inhabitants of Nazareth were somehow deprived. Then, to make matters worse, Nazareth is a basin—a veritable hole in the ground. Nathanael may have reasoned that if "nothing good" had come out of Nazareth in all of that time, why would Jesus' coming from Nazareth change that?

Jesus of Nazareth

I am sure that Jesus would have known the reputation that Nazareth had among its neighboring Galilean cities. He would have known how much contempt the mere mention of Nazareth would have garnered among Galileans. He, no doubt, had encountered others who had expressed their immediate yet unfounded disdain for Him for no other reason than they knew that He lived in Nazareth. It seems that Philip, too, had "heard it all before" based on how he responded to Nathanael questioning whether any good thing could come out of Nazareth. Philip, who, like Nathanael, was from Galilee but not from Nazareth, did not argue with Nathanael, because he knew that it would defeat his purpose - sharing the message of the advent of the Messiah. Philip instead responded by saying, "*...Come and see*" (John 1:46).

Philip responded as he did because he knew who Jesus was ("*.... him, of whom Moses in the law, and the prophets, did write, Jesus of Nazareth, the son of Joseph*" [John 1:45 d-g]). He had complete faith in Jesus and knew that if Nathanael would merely "come and see" - "*O taste and see that the LORD is good...* "(Psalms 34:8a) - that Jesus would prove Himself to Nathanael; even if Jesus did live in Nazareth, He would show Himself to be The Messiah. Philip rested in the fact that He knew who Jesus was and in the fact that Jesus knew Who He was.

And, Jesus knew who Nathanael was. In John 1:47 as Jesus approached Nathanael, He said, "*.... Behold an Israelite indeed, in whom is no guile!*" Jesus knew who Nathanael was because Jesus saw him in the Spirit realm; he saw Nathanael - *Gift of God* - and knew that Nathanael would be one of his disciples. Jesus addressed Nathanael as "***Israelite***", which was a term of high honor and respect. He then told Nathanael that He knew that Nathanael was a man of no guile; he could see Nathanael's spirit.

No longer thinking of Jesus as a mere "man from Nazareth," Nathanael was now curious about Jesus. Because Jesus spoke to him out of His Spirit, it reached Nathanael's spirit (Psalms 42:7). Nathanael then asked Jesus how did Jesus know him. Jesus further revealed to Nathanael that he saw him sitting under a fig tree before Philip approached Nathanael. Remember that Philip saw and approached Nathanael first, having arrived before Jesus did. So, then, whatever happened before Philip got there also had to have happened prior to Jesus' arrival. When Nathanael understood this, Philip's words to him about who Jesus was became rhema. Instantly, he knew that Jesus was *"...the Son of God; thou art the King of Israel."* (John 1:49c-d) All Nathanael's thoughts of Jesus not being the Messiah simply because he came from Nazareth were disproved because Jesus' True Identity had been revealed to him!

Nazareths

God said to not let your Nazareth—your ***unsavory, unfavorable* past**—cause you to remain silent. No matter what the circumstances of your past, God called you from the foundations of the earth. Some people may have come from a troubled home, with parents who were alcoholics or drug addicts. Your family might have been known as the poor family in town, who received public assistance and food stamps, and you were teased about it as a child. Maybe your mother was unwed and had children by a few different men so that no two children in the household had the same father. Or, perhaps you yourself committed adultery or fornication with a minister or other person of prominence and the act became public knowledge. Perhaps you have been falsely accused of something that has been widely broadcast and, no matter how hard you have tried, you cannot prove your innocence and, with the deed being etched in the memories of those around you, you are afraid that it will live on forever in infamy.

It is not that you think you have not been forgiven for any wrongdoings, God said, but it is the ***shame*** and ***embarrassment*** that you associate with the Nazareth that keeps you silent. When you would consider ministering or walking in your calling, the enemy comes and brings you thoughts of the shame and embarrassment that people's reaction to the Nazareth causes you. Before long, you shut down and do nothing. When this happens, your giftings and callings are being silenced.

Jesus never sinned (I Peter 2:22), and yet he was associated with all of the negativity and amorality of Nazareth because of the mere fact that He lived there. He could have gotten upset or displayed a bad attitude because He was being thought of as guilty by association. But, He did not allow the stigma of living in Nazareth to keep him from being about his Father's business (Luke 2:49). When Nathanael responded as he did to Philip, Jesus could have been ashamed or embarrassed to be associated with Nazareth and in His shame He could have neglected to minister to Nathanael. But, Jesus saw the bigger picture.

He saw that the work that He had to do with and in Nathanael was more important than what Nathanael or anyone else thought about him. He also saw that if He did what He was supposed to do - minister to Nathanael - what would happen is instead of **thinking** "Nazareth", Nathanael would **see and hear** God! And, in seeing and hearing God—in *really* receiving a rhema revelation from God—Nathanael would see who Jesus really was - the Son of God. Preconceived notions were dispelled because Jesus walked in who He was - with power and authority - and Nathanael was won to Kingdom building immediately.

God said that shame and embarrassment that we associate with Nazareth come to silence us. Ironically, the very thing that breaks the bondage that that shame and embarrassment have over is not remaining silent! Paul said, *"...but what I hate, that I do"* (Romans 7:15d). He was referring to doing something that is contrary to the Will of God for his life. However, in order to gain victory over the shame and embarrassment that we associate with Nazareth, we have to apply the same mentality, but in reverse. That is, we have to **not** remain silent in our giftings and callings when the shame and embarrassment associated with Nazareth try to silence us. We have to do this with full knowledge of our God-given power and authority (Luke 10:19). He said to remember who you are in Him (Deuteronomy 28:13). Know what He has called you to do (II Timothy 4:2) and what He has said about you (Jeremiah 29:11). Move under the direction of the Holy Spirit and in God's Timing. When we do this, the bondages of shame and embarrassment about Nazareth will be destroyed. We will then be as Jesus—another "good thing" that came out of Nazareth.

---

3 "Nazareth." *Unger Bible Dictionary.* 3rd ed. 1966

Thorns

The word ***silent*** cannot be spelled without the *t*, and a book about factors that can cause our giftings and callings to be silenced would not be complete without a discussion of thorns. Specifically, it is the thorns in our flesh as discussed by the Apostle Paul in II Corinthians 12:1-10 that sometimes cause us to keep silent. Paul's account of the thorn in his flesh is as follows:

It is not expedient for me doubtless to glory. I will come to visions and revelations of the Lord.

I knew a man in Christ above fourteen years ago, (whether in the body, I cannot tell; or whether out of the body, I cannot tell: God knoweth;) such an one caught up to the third heaven.

And I knew such a man, (whether in the body, or out of the body, I cannot tell: God knoweth;)

How that he was caught up into paradise, and heard unspeakable words, which it is not lawful for a man to utter.

Of such an one will I glory: yet of myself I will not glory, but in mine infirmities.

For though I would desire to glory, I shall not be a fool; for I will say the truth: but now I forbear, lest any man should think of me above that which he seeth me to be, or that he heareth of me.

And lest I should be exalted above measure through the abundance of the revelations, there was given to me a **thorn in the flesh**, *the messenger of Satan to buffet me, lest I should be exalted above measure.*

For this thing I besought the Lord thrice, that it might depart from me.

And he said unto me, My grace is sufficient for thee: for my strength is made perfect in weakness. Most gladly therefore will I rather glory in my infirmities, that the power of Christ may rest upon me.

Therefore I take pleasure in infirmities, in reproaches, in necessities, in persecutions, in distresses for Christ's sake: for when I am weak, then am I strong.

WHAT IS A THORN IN THE FLESH?

The word *thorn* in this passage comes from the Greek word *skolops*. It means, *"a pointed piece of wood, a pale, a stake, a sharp stake, a splinter."* Paul was comparing whatever he was experiencing to that of being stabbed constantly or jabbed by a very sharp splinter.

Much has been written on Paul's thorn in the flesh and many have attempted to settle on a definitive definition of it. I prayed about this and God showed me that, for purposes of this chapter, a *thorn in the flesh* is defined as ***"anything that God chooses not to remove from the Believer's life and causes prolonged, chronic, unrelenting spiritual pain and discomfort for the Believer."*** There are physical thorns in the flesh and spiritual thorns in the flesh. Physical thorns in the flesh can be illnesses, painful conditions or any ailment that is chronic. Spiritual thorns in the flesh are areas of spiritual vulnerability to sin that may lead to sinful acts.

Spiritual thorns in the flesh have the potential of inhibiting our relationship with the Lord because spiritual thorns in the flesh are areas of sin. Even physical thorns of the flesh can inhibit our relationship with the Lord because they, too, can lead us into sin. This is because if we are not careful, we allow concentrating on the pain or ailment of a physical thorn in the flesh to distract us from serving God as we should, which is a sin (not serving God means that we are serving something else, even if we are serving physical pain; that becomes idolatry and idolatry is a sin [I Corinthians 10:14]). As we learned Chapter L: Little Foxes, sin in any form separates us from God. Paul understood this when he said the following:

> *Who shall separate us from the love of Christ? shall tribulation, or distress, or persecution, or famine, or nakedness, or peril, or sword?*
>
> *As it is written, For thy sake we are killed all the day long; we are accounted as sheep for the slaughter.*
>
> *Nay, in all these things we are more than conquerors through him that loved us.*
> *38 For I am persuaded, that neither death, nor life, nor angels, nor principalities, nor powers, nor things present, nor things to come,*
>
> *Nor height, nor depth, nor any other creature, shall be able to separate us from the love of God, which is in Christ Jesus our Lord.* – **Romans 8:35-39**

Paul – who had been a persecutor of Christians in his former life (he calls himself the [former] messenger of Satan in II Corinthians 12:7) – had come to know and cherish the Grace of God on his life. His staunch determination about not allowing anything to separate him from the love of God was such that he would allow nothing to get between God and him; and that "nothing" included the thorn in his flesh!

Paul's Thorn: Physical or Spiritual?

There has been much speculation about what Paul's thorn in the flesh was. Some people believe that it was a physical illness or ailment. They say this is evident in the fact that he uses the word *infirmity* many times in the above passage. Paul in his writings made many comparisons between the Body of Christ and a physical body (I Corinthians 12). People who believe that the thorn in his flesh was a physical one say the comparisons could have been because he was ailing in his own body and had reflected much on the "schisms" in it.

Typically, the word *infirmities – asthenesia* in the Greek – is used to denote physical ailments (*"want of strength, weakness and infirmity as relates to the body"* is the first definition in the Greek). But, the word *asthenesia* – also denotes *a want of strength, weakness and infirmity* as it relates to the soul. Therefore, while some people believe that Paul's thorn in the flesh referenced a physical ailment or illness, others believe that Paul was speaking of a spiritual malady.

People who believe that Paul's thorn in the flesh references a spiritual malady rather than a physical ailment cite his use of II Corinthians 2:10 in which he says that he not only takes pleasure in infirmities, but *"in reproaches, in distresses (and) in persecutions for Christ's sake"*. They say that while infirmities may denote a physical ailment, reproaches, distresses and persecutions are not physical illnesses. They are instead spiritual problems. Therefore, these people argue, Paul's thorn in the flesh was spiritual.

These people also believe that Paul's discourse in Romans 7 supports the idea that his thorn in the flesh is spiritual. Romans 7:14-18 says the following:

For we know that the law is spiritual: but I am carnal, sold under sin.

For that which I do I allow not: for what I would, that do I not; but what I hate, that do I.

If then I do that which I would not, I consent unto the law that it is good.

Now then it is no more I that do it, but sin that dwelleth in me.

For I know that in me (that is, in my flesh,) dwelleth no good thing: for to will is present with me; but how to perform that which is good I find not.

People who believe that Paul's thorn in the flesh was spiritual say that the "wrestling" with sin depicted in the above passage is proof that whatever was bothering Paul was spiritual and not physical.

I will share my opinion of whether I believe Paul's thorn in the flesh was physical or spiritual later in this chapter. But, whatever it was - physical or spiritual - the thorn in the flesh caused Paul so much discomfort until he asked the Lord to remove it three times (II Corinthians 12:8). God did not remove it any of those times and Paul learned to live with that thorn in his flesh. He continued to serve God with the thorn yet intact. I gleaned a lot from Paul's story as I have dealt with my own thorns in the flesh - physical and spiritual - this past year.

My Physical Thorns

Readers may recall that in Chapter S: Scared I shared that I was diagnosed with thyroid cancer a year ago (May 2009) and, as a result, I opted to have a thyroidectomy to remove the cancer and to eliminate the chances of any more cancerous thyroid forming. But, in doing so, I risked permanent vocal cord damage. God blessed me to come through the surgery with voice intact. However, while my vocal cords on the left side are getting stronger and stronger, they are not as strong as the used to be. And, whenever seasonal allergies flare up, the vocal cords get weaker; my voice gets somewhat shaky. Even when there are no allergies, there are days when I sing and I can hear my voice going off-key, a problem I never had prior to the thyroidectomy.

Additionally, unless the Lord does a miracle and re-grows my thyroid, I will have no naturally produced hormones in my body and will take a Synthroid tablet or some other hormone replacement therapy tablet every day for the rest of my life. If God does not heal these areas, my vocal cords and my non-existent natural hormones would be my physical thorns in my flesh.

My Spiritual Thorns

In addition to going through the thyroid cancer ordeal this past year, I also went through a spiritual ordeal. I experienced a lot of spiritual warfare in the area of gossip, lies and hurtful things being said about me by people with whom I was at one time extremely close and with whom I shared my innermost heart. It hurt that these people had no remorse for treating me so badly during a very traumatic time in my life; it hurt me more than words can describe. While it hurt me that people who were close to me were responsible for inflicting such great pain, it occurred to me that what made this situation even more painful is that I felt **rejected**; again. Rejection is certainly a spiritual thorn for me.

Lesson Learned from My Thorns

Going through both the physical and emotional troubles all at once was really an eye-opener for me. Prior to the diagnosis of cancer, I would have allowed myself to get stressed out by the fear of rejection—***the spiritual thorn***—and would have gotten extremely upset. But, with the thyroid gone and the hormones in flux, my emotions were harder to handle. This time, instead of just getting upset, I had an anxiety attack! My heart palpitated, I had shortness of breath, my arms and hands trembled: all of this after an argument with one of the people who had caused me pain during this time and who had rejected me. I had never had an anxiety attack before; but it was an eye-opener for me! I felt as if I were going to die!

And, it occurred to me that if God had allowed me to go through cancer and have my thyroid removed and the cancer did not kill me, then I sure was not going to allow rejection to kill me! So, then, my physical thorn in the flesh became the wakeup call for how I allowed the spiritual thorn in the flesh to wreak havoc in my life. Ever since that day, I have changed! I still have the physical thorn; I still experience the fear of rejection (the spiritual thorn in the flesh). But, how I choose to handle the thorns is different.

Since then, the fear of rejection has flared back up many times, especially during my writing time (the enemy replays the painful conversations in my mind while I am trying to write). But, now, whenever I consider "going there" when I am rejected, I remember that panic attack and that feeling of being so close to death (I may not have died from it, but I felt like I would have) and I take measures to ensure that the spiritual thorn in the flesh does not bother me as much. I pray, I rebuke it, and stay focused on my writing. I know that the enemy attacks me in the area while I am writing because he wants to silence me. I keep writing, pressing into God and remaining steadfast in the work of the Lord (I Corinthians 15:58). Before long, I am not feeling as rejected, nor am I having any physical side effects from becoming anxious about being rejected.

Based on my own experiences with thorns in my flesh, I believe that Paul's thorn in the flesh may have been both a physical thorn and the spiritual thorn. I do not know what Paul's specific physical thorn in the flesh would have been. But, it is possible that ***Paul's spiritual thorn in the flesh*** was "**glorying, being exalted": pride**. I say this because he kept making mention of not wanting to glory or to be exalted (II Corinthians 12:1 and II Corinthians 12:6). And, because of this, God may have allowed the physical thorn in the flesh to continuously torment Paul to keep him prayerful so that he would not be apt to give in to pride, his possible spiritual thorn in the flesh.

THORN TOWN

When I think of a person who has experienced an almost unfathomable amount of physical pain in her life, it is my best friend, prophetic intercessor Adrian Thornton. In fact, it seems that ***Adrian's thorn in the flesh is pain itself***. Adrian, who is a female but whose first name is spelled like the masculine spelling of the name, is a shining example of someone who continues to serve God despite the thorn in her flesh. Ironically, Adrian's last name is Thornton. Thornton is of Old English origin and literally means, *"The town of Thorn"* or *"Thorn Town."* Adrian has endured great amounts of pain over large sections of her body, yet she is diligent in waking up at the break of dawn (sometimes staying up all night) and praying and interceding. She reads her Bible faithfully and is available to minister practically 24 hours a day. She has not allowed her thorn in the flesh - pain - to silence her gifting or calling. A synopsis of her testimony is as follows:

In March 1976, 21-year-old Adrian was excited and awaiting being shipped out to Army Basic Training. She was in her car taking care of some business matters before she left when a driver in another car hit her car. This wreck startled her,. At the time, she did not know if she was hurt or not, but she did not want anything to cause her to miss her date for shipping out for the armed forces. She did not report the accident nor did she seek medical treatment. It was also around this time that God had begun dealing with Adrian about developing a closer relationship with him. Prior to becoming an adult, Adrian attended her family's church. But, God was wooing her to get closer to Him and was leading her to find another church home, one which would meet her new spiritual needs. She found one such church. When she visited this church, the Spirit of the Lord would move upon her when she heard the lyrics to the spiritual songs they sang there.

In December 1976 while in the Army, Adrian tore her knee muscles (medial meniscus) in her left knee while trying to jump over a creek as part of a training exercise. Her boots were wet, and her foot slipped. After the surgery, Adrian would, while walking, inadvertently shift the weight that she would have put on the then-sore left knee to the right knee. This resulted in Adrian experiencing excruciating residual pain in the right knee in 1977. She then had to have an additional surgery on the left knee later that year. During this time, she started having spiritual experiences. She would wake up in the middle of the night and read the Word. She had visitations, which made her afraid because she had never experienced anything like that before.

Adrian was discharged from the Army and got a job working at the post office. More than 90 percent of her job at the post office involved standing for long periods of time and lifting heavy packages. In 1979, Adrian had back pain while on her job at the post office. Rather than go to the doctor, she opted to take over-the-counter pain meds and keep working. Unfortunately, by the early 1980's the knee pain flared up again. With the pain mounting and becoming unbearable, Adrian relented and went to the Veteran's Administration Clinic for help. At this time, Adrian—now in her early 30's—was diagnosed with osteoporosis (at the time she thought the diagnosis only applied to her knee; she would learn later that it applied to her back, also).

In mid-to-late 1980's, Adrian experienced severe bunion pain. She speculates that her having to wear ill-fitting boots while in the military may have been the culprit. The result was that in May 1988, Adrian had to have bilateral (the first toes on both feet) bunionectomies (bone is shaved off the sides of both feet) and metatarsal osteotomies (a procedure in which a cut is made in between the first two toes and the first two toes on both feet are broke and reset) In March 1989 a second surgery had to be done on one foot (she does not remember which one; she said it is all a blur). This time, doctors had to take bone out of the hip and put it in that foot. During this process, she had to have screws and pins put in both feet.

And, just as she was recuperating, a man dropped a heavy box on her foot!

In July 1989 – the month of Adrian's 35th birthday – one of the screws in her foot shifted and was protruding down toward the sole of the foot, so that when she walked it would stick her and cause a great amount of pain (this became a literal metal thorn in her flesh). She complained to the doctor about this, but was told that it was, "all in her head." Shortly, it was determined that it was not all in her head and surgery was scheduled. The doctors decided to remove the screw altogether, rather than correct its positioning. Adrian said that it was at this time that she cried out the Lord about the pain that she was experiencing. Like Paul, she, too, was questioning ***why*** she had to go through this. She said that while reading her Bible, she read II Corinthians 12 and God spoke to her what He spoke to Paul: "My Grace is sufficient for thee!"(II Corinthians 12:9). It was not easy, she said, be she learned to be at peace with this and find solace in God's Grace, despite the excruciating pain.

Adrian had been released from her job at the post office because of the pain. She spent most days in pain and going back and forth to the doctor for treatment.

During this time while she was still in severe pain from the knees, back and feet maladies, a doctor haphazardly snatched the pins out of one of her feet (he used too much force). This act resulted in Adrian experiencing nerve damage: specifically, the doctor's action caused Adrian to suffer from Reflex Sympathetic Dystrophy Syndrome (RSDS). RSDS affects part of the sympathetic nervous system, which controls involuntary movement.

In the 1990's the back, knee and foot pain grew progressively worse affecting other areas of her life. In the early 1990's, Adrian had to get injections in her feet for pain. She also continued to get treatments for her back. It is at this time during one such treatment that she found out she had gotten whiplash from the car wreck she had in 1976 and had it all that time (for nearly 20 years).

In 1996, Adrian was in a severe car wreck. The impact aggravated the knee, back and foot ailments all over again. In 1997, in addition to the pain she had already experienced, she began experiencing waves of severe and incapacitating pain all over her body. At this time, Adrian was diagnosed with chronic pain. She said that the pain was debilitating at this point. She felt as if she could feel the earth spinning. The pain made her pray! Her prayer life increased; she prayed during this time as never before!

A year later in 1998, Adrian received another diagnosis - peripheral neuropathy. At this time, she was blessed to meet and be treated by a doctor who had himself been diagnosed and treated for RSDS. In fact, this doctor, who had been a surgeon, had to leave his surgery practice and go into private practice because of his condition. He was sensitive to Adrian's pain and gave her a new medication: He put her on Neurontin. Adrian was thankful because, while the Neurontin did not cure her, it did offer her some relief from the chronic pain (she said at times her brain would burn because pain would move up her body to her brain), relief that she had not had prior to the Neurontin, as the other medications previously described did not significantly decrease her pain.

In 1999, Adrian slipped and fell in Eckerd's drug store and aggravated her back and tore her rotator cuff; she eventually had surgery on the rotator cuff. More pain!

When I met Adrian in about 2001, we were at a church we both attended. She would use a walker to get around in the sanctuary. She was medicated all the time and borderline incoherent. She wore a back brace and because of the medications and would slur her words when she spoke. I did not know all of her story then, but I knew that she was a true Woman of God and had a desire to be in the

House of the Lord because she pressed her way and came on in, despite her condition.

As time went on, Adrian and I became friends. Adrian served as an intercessor at the church. But, she and I became friends outside of the church. She would share bits and pieces of her story with me and I would be in awe of how far God had brought her. According to doctors, she was never supposed to be able to walk again (without the aid of a walker). And, with the medications she was on (one in particular was Doxepin), she was not always completely lucid, sounding sleepy when we would talk on the phone. But, she kept getting better and better. And, she kept interceding and praying.

She shared that there is not a day in her life that she does not experience pain. She said that when she was at her lowest, she cried out to the Lord to "get stuff straightened out." She said she knew that she was up against something that she could not handle. She kept her mind filled with the Word, be it listening to sermons on cassette tapes or reading. And, she prayed regularly.

While Adrian still experiences chronic pain, it is not to the extent that it once was. In 2005, the Spirit of the Lord moved at a church service, and Adrian received a Divine Healing for her back! She is still standing for God - ***even after more than 30 years of being in pain daily*** - and still praying and interceding! She no longer uses a walker and gets around independently. She also does not have to take as much medication as she once did, so that she speaks clearly (we talk on the phone all the time, for long periods of time) and is as sharp as a tack.

She could have allowed her condition to cause her to feel sorry for herself and to give up, but she did not. She pressed past the pain and onto what God had in store for her which, in her words, is a "fasted life" and one of prophetic intercession. When I went through my bout with cancer it was Adrian - still in pain, mind you, but doing better than she was years ago - who encouraged me in the Lord. She spoke words of faith into my spirit and always made me mindful to speak healing over myself. She is an inspiration to me and is an example of what we can do for the Lord, even with and in spite of our thorns in the flesh.

TAKING INVENTORY OF OUR THORNS

I pray that sharing both my story and Adrian's story regarding our thorns in the flesh will motivate the reader to take inventory of his or her own thorn. Some readers may have a physical thorn in the flesh, while other readers may have spiritual thorns in the flesh. While I have chosen to share mine and Adrian has permitted me to share hers, thorns are, in fact, personal. That being said, unless God leads one to share, the thorn in the flesh does not have to be disclosed to anyone but God.

However, I do encourage the reader to be introspective and then be honest with himself or herself. Once the thorn is detected, discerned and named (much like "naming the when" in Chapter 9 of *When*), the reader can then pray about it. Should God choose to remove it from your life, it is no longer a thorn and no longer stands to silence the gifting or calling on your life. However, if, like Paul, you pray about it and God does not remove it, it is intended to serve as a reminder of God's Sovereignty and Man's frailty. Allow the thorn in the flesh to keep you in remembrance of God's Grace in your life. Like Paul's thorn, the thorns in our flesh will provoke us to cry out to God. As we cry out to Him, He opens up the heavens to us and we receive grace and revelation to fulfill our Divine Purposes.

Conclusion

THE SILENCE OF THE LIMBS

"WHEN I KEPT SILENCE, MY BONES WAXED OLD THROUGH MY ROARING ALL THE DAY LONG." – **PSALMS 32:3**

Writing ***I Kept Silence*** – book two in the ***Roaring All the Day Long*** series – has been a joyous undertaking for me. On the heels of a thyroid cancer diagnosis and recovery process, I am excited to know that, despite what the enemy meant to do, the events of the past year neither silenced nor constrained my giftings and callings. Praise be to God that I can still write, sing, preach, teach, counsel and prophesy; actually, I am moving in an even greater measure of anointing now! God is faithful (Lamentations 3:23). He watches over His Word to perform it! He has made many promises to me concerning my ministry and destiny. He told me that I would write and that I would own a successful publishing company, publishing my own works and the works of others. As of this writing, I have two authors signed on whose books my company - ONOMA Ministries & Publications - will soon be publishing!

He is also faithful in giving me the subjects of all the chapters in this book, including this one, "The Silence of the Limbs". In fact, God gave me this chapter and the bulk of its contents and its layout nine years ago (2001), immediately after the first publication of ***When***. God spoke to me and told me that we are His Trees of Righteousness. He then led me to look up the following passage of scripture (Isaiah 61):

The Spirit of the Lord GOD is upon me; because the LORD hath anointed me to preach good tidings unto the meek; he hath sent me to bind up the brokenhearted, to proclaim liberty to the captives, and the opening of the prison to them that are bound;

To proclaim the acceptable year of the LORD, and the day of vengeance of our God; to comfort all that mourn;

To appoint unto them that mourn in Zion, to give unto them beauty for ashes, the oil of joy for mourning, the garment of praise for the spirit of heaviness; that they might be called **trees of righteousness**, *the planting of the LORD, that he might be glorified.*

And they shall build the old wastes, they shall raise up the former desolations, and they shall repair the waste cities, the desolations of many generations.

And strangers shall stand and feed your flocks, and the sons of the alien shall be your plowmen and your vinedressers.

But ye shall be named the Priests of the LORD: men shall call you the Ministers of our God: ye shall eat the riches of the Gentiles, and in their glory shall ye boast yourselves.

For your shame ye shall have double; and for confusion they shall rejoice in their portion: therefore in their land they shall possess the double: everlasting joy shall be unto them.

For I the LORD love judgment, I hate robbery for burnt offering; and I will direct their work in truth, and I will make an everlasting covenant with them.

And their seed shall be known among the Gentiles, and their offspring among the people: all that see them shall acknowledge them, that they are the seed which the LORD hath blessed.

I will greatly rejoice in the LORD, my soul shall be joyful in my God; for he hath clothed me with the garments of salvation, he hath covered me with the robe of righteousness, as a bridegroom decketh himself with ornaments, and as a bride adorneth herself with her jewels.

For as the earth bringeth forth her bud, and as the garden causeth the things that are sown in it to spring forth; so the Lord GOD will cause righteousness and praise to spring forth before all the nations.

We - the People of God— are the "they" referenced in the passage. We are the Trees of Righteousness! But, what is a tree of righteousness and, even more specifically, what is a tree?

"THIS IS A TREE!"

Adrian, whose testimony I shared in Chapter T: Thorns, is a prophetic intercessor, but she also has a healing ministry and a teaching ministry. One day, when I was talking to her on the phone, God showed me her in a vision. Adrian has a beautiful home in an affluent neighborhood. The lawns are meticulously landscaped and many different types of trees grow there. In the vision, I saw Adrian walking down the street in front of her house. Behind her was a group of five - one or two men and the rest women. Apparently, they had walked the length of the block and were headed toward Adrian's house, which sits on the corner. In the vision, Adrian was pointing to various things and telling the people what they were. I could not hear all of it, but the part that I did hear was Adrian pointing to a mesquite tree in her yard and telling the group, "**This *is a tree***!" The group was so impressed by this fact; they ooo'ed and ahh'ed over this simple revelation!

God then showed me that this was a vision that foretold some key information about Adrian's teaching ministry. God said that He would be sending her people who were not ready to handle deep revelations - strong meat (Hebrews 5:14). It is questionable whether these people would even be able to handle the milk of the word (Hebrews 5:13). After all, these were adults who did not know what a tree was; apparently, they had never seen or heard of a tree in their lives! These people would have little to no exposure concerning prophetic revelation; their spiritual knowledge would be almost nil. But, God would use Adrian to teach these people foundational truths to prepare their minds and spirits to receive greater revelations at a later time. From that day forward, whenever we discussed a situation in which the level of revelation was at a babe/milk in the Lord level, we would use the phrase, "**This *is a tree***."

As I was preparing to write this chapter, I thought about this phrase. Although it has that particular meaning for Adrian and me because of the vision the Lord gave concerning her teaching ministry, the truth of the matter is that real trees are quite complex organisms; there is nothing "milk level" about them. Admittedly, my knowledge of botany - the study of plants - is not the best. I prayed that the Lord would not require me to gain the knowledge of a tree surgeon to be able to write this chapter. As it turned out, He only required me to research a few definitions, the first of which is the definition for tree, listed below:

> *"a woody perennial plant, typically having a single stem or trunk growing to a considerable height and bearing lateral branches at some distance from the ground."*

The inner workings of a tree (how it gets water from its roots through the trunk, up and to the leaves; how the leaves give off oxygen and take in carbon dioxide; how a process of photosynthesis occurs causing the leaves to be green and/or, in autumn, change colors) are fascinating! There are different types of trees, different sizes, shapes and colors of fruit and leaves. There are evergreen trees that flourish in the cold. There are magnolia trees, whose flowers give forth an intoxicating aroma. There are fruit-bearing trees such as apple trees, cherry trees and orange trees. There are oak trees, pine trees, cedar trees whose wood is used to make beautiful furniture. Paper and maple syrup come from trees! Trees are an invaluable natural resource.

And, according to the definition, trees are perennial. Perennial means, *"lasting or existing for a long or apparently infinite time; enduring"*. Trees do not die off in the winter and return in the spring; even though the leaves of many trees change colors and fall in autumn, the tree itself is still alive and growing. The definition also says that a tree has *" a single stem or trunk that grow to a considerable height."* The considerable height is what distinguishes a tree from a bush or a shrub, which is typically "shorter" than a tree. The definition also says that a tree bears *"lateral branches at some distance from the ground."* These branches are higher up than the branches on a bush or scrub and certainly higher that the branches on a vine. Another name for the branches on a tree is limbs.

As we read in Isaiah 61:3, the Bible says speaks of People of the Lord as being Trees of Righteousness. In the passage below, Psalms 1:1-3 also speaks Godly men being trees:

> *Blessed is the man that walketh not in the counsel of the ungodly, nor standeth in the way of sinners, nor sitteth in the seat of the scornful.*
>
> *But his delight is in the law of the LORD; and in his law doth he meditate day and night.*
>
> ***And he shall be like a tree planted by the rivers of water, that bringeth forth his fruit in his season; his leaf also shall not wither; and whatsoever he doeth shall prosper.***

Like trees, we, the Trees of Righteousness (i.e., *"the man that walked not in the counsel of the ungodly, nor standeth in the way of the sinner, nor sitteth in the seat of the scornful"* [verse 1]) we are supposed to be perennial; we are supposed to be "instant in season and out of season (II Timothy 4:2)." We have seasons of growth and flourishing and we have seasons of dormancy and reflection. We have seasons when we can feel the warmth of the fire of the Holy Spirit and we go through seasons when we do not feel it as much; instead of ministering during those times, we "chill" (during our spiritual winters). We have seasons in which we bear much fruit and seasons in which the fruit is not visible to the physical eye, but is yet in the process of being manifested in our lives, because the seed as been planted, watered and cultivated (I Corinthians 3:7). We have roots (Psalms 1:3) and our roots absorb water, the

Word of God. We can grow to "considerable heights" (Psalms 148:1). And, we have branches - limbs! But, what are limbs?

LIMBS

A limb of a tree is defined as, *"a large branch of a tree."* But, there is another definition of limb which means, *"an arm or a leg of a person or a four-legged animal, or a bird's wing."* We know that trees have branches (per the definition of tree). But, can trees have legs? Considering the following passage of scripture:

> *And he cometh to Bethsaida; and they bring a blind man unto him, and besought him to touch him.*
>
> *And he took the blind man by the hand, and led him out of the town; and when he had spit on his eyes, and put his hands upon him, he asked him if he saw ought.*
>
> *And he looked up, and said, I see men as trees, walking.*
>
> *After that he put his hands again upon his eyes, and made him look up: and he was restored, and saw every man clearly.*
>
> *And he sent him away to his house, saying, Neither go into the town, nor tell it to any in the town.* – **Mark 8:22-26**

In this passage of scripture, a blind man was brought to Jesus to receive sight. Jesus took the man out of the town, put spit on the man's eyes and put His Hands upon the man. Jesus then asked the man if he saw Jesus clearly (Mark 8:32). The next verse, Mark 8:24 says that the man who Jesus was healing from blindness saw *"men as trees, walking."*

I have heard this passage preached before and I have heard it said that the man was not completely healed the first time Jesus laid hands upon him and the man was having blurred or distorted vision. In other words, preachers who preach the passage with that interpretation are saying that ***Jesus failed to heal the man the first time and that it took two "tries" for Jesus to get it right***! Jesus failed? The same Jesus who turned water to wine (John 2:1-11); the same Jesus who raised Lazarus from the dead (Mark 5:1-20); the same Jesus who casted the legion of demons from the man (John 11); the same Jesus who, after being crucified for my sins, went down into Hell and took the keys of death ***and then*** rose again—were the preachers talking about ***that*** Jesus? If so, then I think they were sadly mistaken or at least misguided. Jesus did not fail to heal the man on the first undertaking. No, not only did Jesus heal the man's physical eyes, but he opened the man's spiritual eyes as well!

The Lord showed me that when the man saw men as trees walking, he was seeing in the Spirit. He was seeing the "true man" as God intended him: walking out his Prophetic Destiny, abiding in his calling and giftings as a Tree of Righteousness. And, to do this, the trees had to have feet. And, the feet had to be attached to legs!

So, then, spiritually speaking, trees of righteousness have legs. But, what about arms; can trees have arms? Let's explore Isaiah 55:11-12, which reads as follows:

> *For ye shall go out with joy, and be led forth with peace: the mountains and the hills shall break forth before you into singing, and all the* **trees of the field shall clap their hands**.

> *Instead of the thorn shall come up the fir tree, and instead of the brier shall come up the myrtle tree: and it shall be to the LORD for a name, for an everlasting sign that shall not be cut off.*

Verse 12d of this passage says, "*....all the trees of the field shall clap their hands.*" Clapping in this instance is "*an act of striking together the palms of the hands, either once or repeatedly.*" So, then, clapping involves the use of hands. Hands are attached to the body at the wrists. And, the wrists are the lower joint portions of the arms. It would be hard to clap the hands without arms, even if the hands were really huge and the body was small. No, the arms are the connecting appendages - ***the limbs*** - between the hands and the shoulder, which connects the arm to the "trunk" of the body. Without the arms, the hands could not function. If a Tree of Righteousness has hands, then it stands to reason that it must also have arms.

SILENCE

Through this book, we have been discussing the silencing or constraint of a gifting or calling and some possible factors in to our keeping silent. In the Introduction, I gave the definition of *silence* as it pertains to this book. Let us now define *silence* at it appears in the dictionary. Silence is both a verb and a noun. The definition of *silence* as a verb is "*cause to become silent; prohibit or prevent from speaking.*" The definitions of *silence* as a noun are as follows:

- *complete absence of sound*
- *the fact or state of abstaining from speech*
- *the avoidance of mentioning or discussing something*
- *the state of standing still and not speaking as a sign of*

respect for someone deceased or in an opportunity for prayer

God showed me that all of these definitions are applicable to the silence discussed in this book. When we do not allow the Lord to speak through us because we are scared (Chapter S) or because we are so used to using our own imagination until we can't hear Him to get instructions (Chapter I), there is a "*complete absence of sound*" coming from our giftings and callings. When we do not preach or teach because our lives are full of "little" sins and we do not have a relationship with God that we need to have, resulting in our inability to hear Him clearly (Chapter L) or we are overwhelmed with the storms of life and do not operate in our giftings and callings (Chapter E), we are in a "*state of abstaining from speech.*" When we do not walk in our callings because we are held prisoner by shame and embarrassment because of our past (Chapter N) or we do not want to minister because we are too busy focusing on our pains (Chapter T), we are "*avoiding the mentioning or discussing*" what God would say through us, either through our words are deeds.

But, one might ask, what about the fourth definition of silence? And, how does silence pertain to limbs and trees?

Our Spiritual Limbs

Our spiritual limbs - spiritual arms and legs - are our ministries or whatever God has called us to do. Specifically, they are the part of us that extend from ourselves and reach out to do what God has directed us to do. This extension of what is inside of us is the thing that causes us to be able to move "outside of ourselves" and get the things of the Lord done. Returning to Isaiah 61, consider verse six, which reads:

> *But ye shall be named the Priests of the LORD: men shall call you the Ministers of our God: ye shall eat the riches of the Gentiles, and in their glory shall ye boast yourselves.*

After we become Trees of Righteousness (Isaiah 61:3), we then become "*Priests of the LORD*" and "*Ministers of our God.*" As with any tree, the fruit it produces is what is known ***by*** ("*For every tree is known by its own fruit...* "[Luke 6:44a]), **but the ministry is what a Tree of Righteousness is known** ***for***. We may bear fruits of righteousness but ***how we display those fruits and make them available for consumption is what we are known for - our ministries, giftings and callings; our spiritual limbs - display the fruits that we bear.***

For instance, if a person is full of the joy, because joy is one of the Fruits of the Holy Spirit then that person is known by his or her joy. But, **how** do others know that that person has joy? *They can see the joy by how the person displays it.* Maybe she sings praises to God; maybe she ministers joy by encouraging others. Maybe she writes about it. The joy is the fruit, but the singing praises, ministering and writing would be the branches - ***the spiritual limbs.***

Our Spiritual Legs

With our spiritual legs, we execute our "walk." Just as Jesus spoke to Nathanael and beckoned Him to follow and serve (John 1:51), so God speaks to us and beckons us to follow and serve. And, it is with our spiritual legs that we follow! It is our spiritual legs that give power and anchorage to the feet (our spiritual foundation) so that walking is possible!

While a solid foundation is essential to a successful spiritual walk, one cannot benefit from the foundation unless the foundation is utilized. And, in the case of the spiritual feet, one's feet would be useless just sitting there

- "*Faith* (***the receiving and believing of the Word which grows through hearing the preached Word***) *without works* (***works denote doing something with the faith***) *is dead* (James 2:20)." Just as faith without works is dead, feet without legs are "dead"(they are useless unless they are connected and are being used; we cannot use the feet without having legs). So, then our spiritual feet are not functional without our spiritual legs.

The Bible also says for us to"... *be ye doers* (***actively performing the teachings of the Gospel and walking out your calling and ministry***) *of the word, and not hearers only* (***building a foundation through hearing the Word of God***), *deceiving your own selves* [James 1:22])". It is the spiritual legs that provide the power and ability for the "doing" of the Word to take place. They help take us to the place where for which our foundation has been prepared!

A variation of this same idea can be seen in Hebrews 5:12-14, which says the following :

> *For when for the time ye ought to be teachers, ye have need that one teach you again which be the first principles of the oracles of God; and are become such as have need of milk, and not of strong meat.*
>
> *For every one that useth milk is unskilful in the word of righteousness: for he is a babe.*
>
> *But strong meat belongeth to them that are of full age, even those who by reason of use have their senses exercised to discern both good and evil.*

In this passage of scripture, the people are being admonished to not merely sit up and build up a strong spiritual foundation by just listening to sermons and being taught. Instead, at this point in their spiritual walks, instead of being taught, they should be teaching others! Reference is made to the difference between milk and strong meat. The passage suggests that the people to whom this passage was directed should have been past the milk phase and now at the strong meat phase of revelation. But, because they have taken to sitting around and hearing the Word (spiritual feet) but have not utilized or shared the information/revelation they have amassed (their spiritual legs), they were not mature (readers of *When* may recall that such a person was described as a "word junkie" in Chapter 1: The *When* of Prophetic Inquiry). In fact, they are immature and are not ready to serve as teachers or sharers of the Word. They were complacent in using their spiritual legs and now, even if they were called upon, they could not "be instant, in season and out of season (II Timothy 2:4)." ***They were spiritually immature and sluggish.***

When we do not exercise our spiritual legs - ***when we do not* walk *in our callings*** - we become spiritually overweight and sluggish. Many people grow weary in well doing (II Thessalonians 3:13) and stop walking. The enemy tells them that they can take a break - a short rest - and, as long as they get back to whatever God has told them to do at some point, it will be okay. But, prolonged inactivity of our spiritual legs can result in our becoming spiritually overweight. We lose the spiritual agility of not just the legs, but of other parts of our spiritual bodies. So, then, our spiritual legs - our ministries, giftings and callings - yield mobility and power to the feet, but they also enable us to keep the rest of the body fit.

Our Spiritual Arms

Our spiritual arms enable us to reach out to people and to reach up to God. While the hands are the parts of the Body that grasp, the arms must first reach toward what the hands are grasping. So, then the arms provide the hands directionality, guidance and stability.

And, like the spiritual legs provide power for the spiritual feet, the spiritual arms provide power for the spiritual hands. The spiritual arms enable us to embrace hurting people (Ecclesiastes 3:5). They cradle and protect spiritual babes (II Kings 4:15) and are used to hold a bow in times of war and to break the bow of the enemy (II Samuel 22:35). The arms help enable the hands to repel dangers, to clap for praise (Psalms 47:1), to clap for spiritual warfare (Lamentations 2:15), to prepare and feed (others and ourselves) spiritual food (Matthew 14:19), to cleanse ourselves (II Corinthians 7:1), to point and direct (Numbers 34:10), to write the vision and make plain (Habakkuk 2:2). Like the spiritual legs, the spiritual arms are essential parts of the Body because they enable mobility.

Therefore, when our spiritual limbs are not in motion, we are not getting anything done. When they are **still**, we are not ministering. When they are **still**, we are not walking in our callings. When they are **still**, we are not operating in our giftings. **Nothing** ***happens for us or through us when our spiritual limbs are still.***

PLEASE PAUSE NOW FOR A MOMENT OF SILENCE

The fourth definition of silence as a noun is, "*the state of* **standing still** *and* **not speaking** *as a sign of respect for someone deceased or in an opportunity for prayer.*" In other words, ***pausing for a moment of silence***. The concept and practice of pausing for a moment of silence is to pay tribute to and show respect for someone deceased; sometimes people use these moments to pray (usually in a public place where praying aloud is not permitted). While a moment of silence may be appropriate in those instances, ***we should never take a self-imposed moment of silence from walking in our callings and operating in our giftings.***

God showed me that, just as this fourth definition of *silence* says, our spiritual limbs have been "***standing still***" and "***not speaking***" for too long. God showed me that the "moment" of silence is the trick of the enemy sent to keep the Trees of Righteousness from "branching out" into their giftings, callings and ministries. Unfortunately, the "moment" of silence has turned into a lifestyle of silence for some Believers, with the enemy lulling them into a false sense of security that whatever the Lord has called them to do can be done "later." A spirit of procrastination has crept into the Body. But, the time is now ("*To day if ye will hear his voice, harden not your heart...*[Psalms 95:7d-95:8a]), God says, because for some "later" never comes (Luke 12:20). We, as Trees of Righteousness; we, as the Body of Christ, have been guilty of having prolonged periods of being stationary and doing nothing. We have been guilty of not walking in our callings and giftings for extended periods of time. ***God said that we*—the Trees of Righteousness; the Ministers of the Lord—*have had silent limbs.*** But, He said, for those who will hear and obey, the silence is being broken!

THE SILENCE IS BROKEN!!!

God said through the pages of this book and through Words He has ministered directly to your spirit, the silence is being broken. He said that you will begin to receive an unction to minister; to abide in your calling. Do not disallow this unction. It is of Him! Through your obedience God will silence the silencers in your life. As this happens, be prepared to go forth in your calling with more power and authority than ever before.

Be ever cognizant of silencers in the future, as they will surely come to try to keep you from walking in your Divine Purpose. Use spiritual discernment to recognize them and use the Word to keep them at bay. And, whatever you do, keep walking! Walk past the little foxes and walk on the water through the Euroclydon; walk "through the valley of death" and fear no evil. Walk around Nazareth with confidence and near the thorns, knowing they cannot stop you anymore. Let the light of the Word illuminated by the Holy Spirit lead you and you will not have to imagine your path. But, whatever you do, walk, walk, walk. Whatever you do, keep walking! Walk right into your place of Divine Purpose and Destiny!

MY SILENCE IS BROKEN!!!

I am writing this section of the Conclusion with tears of joy in my eyes! It gives me great pleasure and an enormous sense of accomplishment to say that I am now concluding *I Kept Silence*. These are tears of joy because after experiencing a nine-year silence myself (in the area of writing), I have finally done what God told me to do concerning this book and have finished another part of the ***Roaring*** series. And, in doing so, I broke chains and bondages off of myself that I did not even know were there!

I am excited to start writing *My Bones Waxed Old*, book three in the *Roaring* series. I can hardly wait to hear what God will say about our spiritual limbs - spiritual arms and legs - and the bones of which they are comprised. While God has revealed the title and the overall topic of the book to me, He has not yet revealed any specifics about the layout of the book or chapter names. In fact, unlike the chapters in *When* and in *I Kept Silence,* I have no foreknowledge whatsoever what the specific subject matter of any of the chapters will be. I do not know any of the key scriptures that will be discussed. I do not know who will write the foreword. But, what I do know is this: I am flowing more freely than I had in a long time; I am singing praises to God more; I am happier; I am at peace! I am no longer being silenced! I am free!

"You've turned my mourning into dancing again,
You've lifted my sorrows.
I can't stay silent.
I must sing for Your Joy has come!"[4]

"Mourning into Dancing"
Song written and performed by Ron Kenoly

---

[4] Kenoly, R. (1995). *Mourning Into Dancing. On High Places: The Best of Ron Kenoly.* New York. Sony Records.

www.ingramcontent.com/pod-product-compliance
Lightning Source LLC
LaVergne TN
LVHW052338100826
845147LV00020B/1112

* 9 7 8 0 9 7 0 1 1 8 4 2 4 *